MW01378550

With My Best Wishes,
Skip Biron

SKIP'S LEGACY

SKIP'S LEGACY

Edward Biron

Library of Congress Control Number:		2015917941
ISBN:	Hardcover	978-1-5144-1528-3
	Softcover	978-1-5144-1527-6
	eBook	978-1-5144-1526-9

Print information available on the last page

Rev. date: 12/14/2015

To order additional copies of this book, contact:
Xlibris
1-888-795-4274
www.Xlibris.com
Orders@Xlibris.com
726715

CONTENTS

Dedication

I would like to dedicate this book to Melissa who urged me to write my story back in December 2001.

PROLOGUE

As I begin to write the story of my life, I find myself very rapidly approaching my 85th year here on earth; in extremely high spirits and in reasonably good health. I am, however, in a very nostalgic mood, as well. This story is entitled "Skip's Legacy." It is an autobiographical story reflecting my own life, as well as, the times and events which surrounded it. It is an account of the historical events and my own experiences dealing with them from 1930 to the present day. It is a father's legacy: A lasting heritage for my children, grand-children and great grand-children.

I Am From

I am From….
Removing my hat when in a restaurant or in the presence of ladies…
Opening doors and helping little old ladies across the street...
Getting married first and then having the children…
Taking all the food I wanted, then eating all I took (or else!)…
Eating everything in my plate or getting no dessert…
Licking the beaters when Mom was baking…
Getting into the house in the evening when the "street lights" came on…
Drinking water from a garden hose, not a plastic bottle…

I am From….
Sharing a bottle of Moxie with four friends (No one died!)…
Being told, "If you get killed, don't come home to me." …
Calling Policemen and others in authority "Sir"…
Calling rabbits animals, not tiny foreign cars…
Thinking fast food meant for Lent, it didn't come from MacDonald's…
"Making out" meant how I did on an exam in school…
Mowing the grass, not smoking it…
Singing music with meaningful lyrics and a nice melody...

I am From….
Eating beans and hotdogs every Saturday night…
Shooting "Hoops" at a basket mounted on a telephone pole…
Playing "Kick-the-Can & Hide-and-Seek" in the street after supper…
Being taught by school teachers all of whom were unmarried women...
Reciting the Pledge of Allegiance" and Prayer each day at school…
Trying to keep God in our schools and in our government…
Standing at attention, hand on heart when the American flag went by…

Here Are a Few of My Favorite Things!

Sports	Basketball, Softball, Golf
Book	A Tale of Two Cities
Poem	The Touch of the Masters Hand
Leisure Activities	Coin/Stamp Collecting, Carving, Puzzling
Dessert	Chocolate Cream Pie
Author	Mark Twain
Bible Verse	I Corinthians Ch13
Hymns	Be Not Afraid, On Eagle's Wings
Vacation Spots	Aruba, Puerto Vallarta, Mexico
Sports Team	Boston Celtics

Family Portrait

Full Given Name	Edward Joseph Biron Jr. (Skippy)
Date of Birth	September 2, 1930
Place of Birth	Haverhill, MA. USA
Mother's Full Name	Angela Anna Marinaro (Ainge)
Place/Date of Birth	Haverhill, MA USA Nov. 22, 1910
Date of Death	March 27, 1952 (42yrs-4mos-5days)
Father's Full Name	Edward Joseph Biron Sr. (Diddy)
Place/Date of Birth	Exeter, NH USA July 30, 1908
Date of Death	April 10, 2001 (92yrs-8mos-11days)

Maternal Grandparents

Domenico Marinaro	Angela DeSando
San Pietro, Italy 1873-1943	San Pietro, Italy 1873-1928

Paternal Grandparents

George Biron	Olivine Filomena Gagnon
Exeter, NH USA	Sherbrook, Quebec, Canada

Siblings, Places/Dates of Births

Brother—Walter Robert Biron (Buddy)
Haverhill, MA USA November 8, 1935

Sister—Norma Elizabeth Biron
Amesbury, MA USA November 2, 1942

Marriages:

1ST Marriage—Pauline Mary Boisvert (Penny)
Salem, N.H. St. Joseph's Church July 17, 1954

2nd Marriage—Georgette Alice Fortin Sturgis (Jet)
Salem, N.H. Mary, Queen of Peace March 26, 1977

Names & Birth Dates of My Children

Children—

Angela Jeanne Biron	Salem, N.H. January 2, 1956

Step Children—

William Coleman Sturgis	Newburyport, MA April 12, 1947
George Arthur Sturgis	Newburyport, MA July, 2, 1949
Dana Brian Sturgis	Exeter, N.H. February 18, 1964

Military Statistics

Branch of Service:	United States Navy	Serial Number: #7528769
Date Entered:	October 4, 1948	Place: Boston, MA
Date Separated:	September, 18, 1952	Place: San Diego, CA
Discharge Type:		Honorable Discharge
Rank: Radioman 3rd Class (RM3):		War Served: Korean War

Marinaro Family Data

My grandfather, Domenico Marinaro was a tailor in Haverhill, MA for most of his life. His shop was in Currier Square on the ground floor of a triple decker. Today, a funeral parlor is there; Scattamacchia & D'Amico. My mother's funeral was conducted from there in 1952.

My mother, Angela Anna Marinaro, came from a family of 10 children: 4 girls; Elizabeth, Mary Palma, Katherine & Angela and 6 boys; Joseph, Bruno, Jimmy, Dominic, Albert and Columbus.

My aunt, Katherine Marinaro was a school teacher in Haverhill, MA and became the principal at the Tilton Elementary School there.

My uncle, Bruno Marinaro died of influenza during World War I, while serving in the U.S. Navy.

My uncle, Jimmy Marinaro died of a heart attack in 1921 while running across Swazey's Field in Haverhill, MA.

My uncle, Dominic Marinaro was killed on Omaha Beach in Normandy during World War II. He was a marathon runner who ran in both the Boston 26 mile marathon and the 26 mile marathon from Lawrence, MA to Salisbury Beach, MA. back in the early 1940's.

My uncle, Columbus Marinaro (Clum), was a career soldier in the U.S. Army. He was in Hawaii when the Japanese bombed Pearl Harbor on Dec. 7, 1941. He retired from the army after serving 20 plus years. Then he became a Postal Carrier (Mailman) in Haverhill, MA. and retired from the Post Office after many years of service there.

My uncle, Albert Marinaro (Bibs), was a cook in the U.S. Army during World War II. He was in the Coast Artillery, stationed primarily along the New England Coast. He was stationed at Fort Prebble, near Portland, ME, where he met and married my Aunt Muriel who came and helped us care for my sister, Norma, when my mother had problems deriving from her birth.

Biron Family Data

My grandmother, Olivine Gagnon, married my grandfather, George Biron, when she was 15 years old and left a convent in Sherbrooke, Canada to do so. She became a Gold Star Mother during World War II, but she never became a naturalized citizen of the United States.

My father, Edward Biron came from a family of 11 children: 3 girls; Irene, Antoinette (Jeanie) and Rita and 8 boys; Wilfred, Edward, Antonio (Tony), Thomas, Albert, Ralph (Duke), Arthur and George.

He retired from Anchor Hockings in Jacksonville, FL as a Superintendent (Plant Manager). He was the #1 person in charge in a huge glass producing plant there. He had received only a 4th grade education at the Wingate School in Haverhill, MA.; having been forced to leave school at a very early age and go to work in the shoe shops of Haverhill, MA. to help in the support of his family.

My uncle, Tony Byron was in the U.S. Army during World War II and was stationed in North Africa chasing the German General, Rommel, through the desert. He was seriously wounded when he stepped on a mine in combat. He survived his injuries and married one of the nurses, Jenny Bloyder, who cared for him when he returned to the states at the VA Hospital in Northhampton, MA. They had 3 children; my cousins, Billy, Johnny & Maryann.

My uncle, Ralph Byron (Duke), served in the U.S. Army during World War II. He served in Burma, it's called Myanmar now, under General Stillwell.

My uncle, Arthur Byron, was also in the U.S. Army during World War II. He used to take me fishing in the Spicket River in Methuen, MA when I was 10 years old. He was captured in the Philippine Islands by the Japanese and held prisoner. He was killed during the infamous Bataan Death March. His remains have been interred at the Immaculate Conception Cemetery in Lawrence, MA.

My uncle, Wilfred Biron, the "black sheep" of the family. He would disappear for years at a time. He would re-appear only when he needed something. He was the spitting image of my father, so he would come to Haverhill and pretend to be his brother, Diddy (my father) and purchase items; such as, shoes, clothes etc. and charge them to my father's account. There were no credit cards in those days; everyone ran a tab until payday or whenever. We even ran a tab at the corner grocery store; there was no Market Basket or Hannaford's. My Uncle Wilfred would show up, buy something and leave town for years. The only way we knew that he had been around was the trail of unpaid bills that he left behind. I saw my Uncle Wilfred to speak to perhaps 3 or 4 times in my entire life. Rumor has it that he ran off and did a hitch in the Canadian Army during World War II. I would not be surprised. My father always had my Uncle Wilfred's back. He never seemed to be annoyed about paying his brother's bills.

Note:

Notice that some of my father's siblings were named, Biron with an "i" and some were named Byron with a "y." It all depends on which way the doctor or midwife spelled their last name on the birth certificate at city hall when their birth was reported. This fact was unknown until World War II when my Uncles Tony, Duke and Arthur went to city hall to obtain their birth certificates, required when joining the U.S. Army. When each of them learned how their name had been recorded on their birth certificate, they left it that way.

CHAPTER 1

"Born Free"

I was born September 2, 1930 and was Baptized a few days later, in Saint Rita's Church on Reed Street in Haverhill. MA which was still a part of Saint James Church on Winter Street in those days. My God Parents were Johnny Medaglia and my Aunt Jeannie (Biron) Robichaud, my father's sister. My parents were living on Sandler Terrace in a triple decker, but we moved immediately into a first floor, two bedroom flat down the block on Washington Street.

My mother named all three of her children before they were actually born. She called me "Skippy" before I was born. She never doubted that her first born child would be a boy and that I would be named Skippy. I was baptized and legally named Edward Joseph Biron Jr. after my father, of course. Mom did not want to call me "Junior"; I think that was why she decided on Skippy. Five years later, when my brother came along, again having no doubt that her second child would be another boy, she decided he was to be called "Buddy". He was also baptized in Saint Rita's Church and was officially named Walter Robert Biron, after my father's oldest and dearest friend, Walter "Buddy" Wysocki. Skippy was to be Daddy's boy and Buddy was to be Momma's boy. My father had been nicknamed "Diddy" when he was a young man; so we became the Biron Threesome; Diddy, Skippy and Buddy. My sister, Norma, did not come along until I was 12 years old.

As a child, I played usually by myself between the ages of 1 and 5. Living on Washington Street in Haverhill, I would amuse myself by lining up my toys on my bedroom window sill which faced the street. I would show off all my toys to passers by. Meanwhile, in the back yard, which was surrounded by a high wooden fence and a locked gate, I would ride my pedal-propelled automobile for hours. Next door, I was able to watch the construction of a new building; that became the Polish National Home, which was completed in 1936. My brother, Buddy was born while we were living there on November 8, 1935.

CHAPTER 2

"Up a Lazy River"

In 1936, we were still residing on Washington Street in Haverhill. My father was working as a "Hardener" in the Merrimack Hat Shop across the river in Bradford. He walked back and forth to work, a distance of about ½ mile each way. We did not own a car. In the Spring of 1936, the Merrimack River flooded it's banks all the way down through Lowell, Lawrence, Methuen, Haverhill, Amesbury and Newburyport. From our kitchen window, I could see entire buildings and all kinds of debris come floating down the river and get hung up on the old black bridge which spans the Merrimack River. That was a very moving experience, even now, I can still visualize it! The hat shop, where my father was working, was flooded out, as well as the hat shop down river in Amesbury; putting a great many people out of work. There was another plant in Amesbury, well away from the river which was not affected by the flood, called the "fur plant." They moved my father's job to the fur plant in Amesbury and started a night shift in order to keep the operation going. So we moved to Amesbury on Congress Street. My father had to walk about 1 ½ miles each way to get to work. I remember that my father worked very hard. He was on "piece work", which meant he was paid for output; pennies per unit. I remember my mother packing him a lunch every day. She also did a lot of "canning"; we had a huge garden from which she would get the vegetables for preserving. Buddy and I did most of the weeding in the garden.

Life was good. We all seemed to be happy. Everyone looked after one another. Families were very closely knit. The entire family ate three meals a day at the kitchen table. We never locked our doors and doctors made house calls. We had no car, no telephone, no washing machine, no refrigerator and no television. We walked everywhere; to school, to church, to the grocery store, to the movies....everywhere! Sometimes we took the bus to get from one town to another or to go to Salisbury Beach. All young boys my age had two pair of jeans; called "dungarees" then, one pair for every day and one pair for Sunday's best.

So, the Flood of '36 was the reason that we moved from Haverhill to Amesbury. We did not go back to Haverhill until World War II had begun, around 1943.

Between the ages of 6 and 11, I was living in Amesbury on Congress Street and usually played with the neighborhood kids. In the evenings, after supper, when the weather was good, we would play kick-the-can, hide-and-seek, relieveo and dodge-ball in the street "until the street lights came on."

In the winter, I did a great deal of skiing. My father and I did a lot of cross country skiing and sometimes I would ski to school. My father was a marathon runner and the cross country skiing helped him to train in the winter. He belonged to a group of 7 men who used to run road races as a team, including the Boston Marathon and the old Lawrence to Salisbury Beach Marathon. They ran as a group called The Amesbury AC. My Uncle Dom, my mother's brother, would run in these events, as well. I often helped them to train on my bike in the summer and on skis in the winter. When they were running in races, I would station myself along the route and provide them with water and oranges. On cold and rainy days, throughout my entire childhood, we played "board" games on the kitchen table on the underside of the "oil cloth" which normally covered the table. We played Chess, Checkers, Parcheesi, and Backgammon; the layouts for these games were stenciled on the underside of the table covering. It was my job to transfer these layouts each time my mother purchased a new oil cloth. Sometimes my cousin, Jan, would come and visit for a week or two in the summer. We had no guest room, so she slept between Buddy and me, in the same bed. Buddy was 2 years old; cousin Jan and I were 7 or 8. I amused them by making shadows on the ceiling, that looked like animals, with my hands and the light that came from the other room. Jan was the very first person I ever knew that slept with her eyes open. How eerie is that? We would be talking and playing in bed and all of a sudden, she would not respond, but her eyes remained open all night long.

CHAPTER 3

"Stormy Weather"

In 1938, a hurricane came through the valley. Back then, they did not name hurricanes after men and women. There wasn't much of a warning in those days. We had no television or telephone; just an old Adwater Kent vacuum tube radio which we used only in the evenings and on weekends. That day, I was out in the meadow flying my home made kite; made out of newspaper and rags, when my Mom called me to come inside. "Skippy, there is a storm coming," she said, "Come in!" I had been thinking that the winds were up because I had no trouble getting that kite aloft, but now I was having a great deal of difficulty bringing it down. So, I was forced to cut it loose. When I finally came into the house, I remember saying to myself; "That kite must be in Canada by now."

When I was a boy of 8 or 9 years of age, living on Congress Street in Amesbury; my Grandfather Biron, my father and I were heavily engaged with the breeding, raising and training of gamecocks. Today, people have an entirely different attitude concerning cock fighting than they did back in 1930's; it is currently considered cruel and abusive treatment of animals. Cock fighting is said to be the oldest spectator sport in the world; it goes back 6,000 years in Persia.

Today, cock fighting is illegal in all 50 of the U.S. states and the District of Columbia but it remains legal in the U.S. territories of Puerto Rico, the U.S. Virgin Islands, the Northern Mariana's and Guam. Cock fighting was allowed in many states; such as, Florida, Georgia, Texas, Alabama, and Louisiana until 2007. Louisiana was the last state to ban the fighting of roosters in June, 2007.

Gamecocks possess congenital aggression toward all males of the same species; they are born and bred to fight. They are trained, prepared and conditioned, much like race horses or professional athletes. While in training, the birds are equipped with 2 leather pouches; that look like boxing gloves placed over the their spurs, which have been cut short. In an actual fight, the leather pouches are replaced by a set of very sharp, steel spurs. The roosters are paired off to fight according to their body weight. Wagers are frequently made on the outcome of the match.

Our gamecocks were bred especially for their strength, stamina and refusal to stop fighting and flee the pit. Our brood cock was a grey, named "Tarzan" ; who had won many fights before he was put out with the hens to fertilize their eggs. Tarzan was the source of the Biron game cock pedigree. The next in line was "Flash," who also became a brood cock.

We also had a very good cock fighter; whose name was, "One Eye Connelly," who won lots of fights even after he lost an eye to a steel spur in battle. He would continuously circle his opponent counter clock-wise to keep his good eye on his adversary. I "adopted" a small, brown red cock that no one wanted and I named him, "Robin." I asked my father if I could raise and train him to fight. He said, "OK," but it was hard to find a match for him, he was so small. I put some weight on him, kept him in condition and Robin ultimately won 13 fights before I retired him.

In those days, the breeders of gamecocks from Massachusetts were always competing with those from New Hampshire; each having their own handler and venue. It is necessary to have a good "handler" in the pit; the handler can make the difference whether a cock fight was won or lost. My father was the handler for all owners from Mass. and our "home court" was a cock pit in the woods of Georgetown, Mass., while Seabrook, N.H. was the local venue for the N.H. owners. We moved back to Haverhill in 1942 and no longer had room for gamecocks; we gave all our roosters and cock fighting paraphernalia to a man named, Georgie Edmunds, another Mass. breeder who owned a large spread of land in Salisbury Plains. Georgie was the school bus driver for the Town of Amesbury. In those days, parochial school children could not ride to school in the school bus, only public school kids were allowed. That was a very controversial issue when I was a kid growing up. It wasn't until the late 40's or early 50's that all the city and town governments in the area voted to allow both public and parochial school children to ride the school buses.

I remember that my father subscribed to two very popular cock fighting magazines; the "Feathered Warrior" and "Grit and Steel." They did not stop publishing those two magazines until 2007, abandoning many disgruntled readers. Keep in mind also that the University of South Carolina and Jacksonville State University in Alabama both have a gamecock as their mascot.

I once owned a beautiful, mating pair of snow white Fantail Pigeons. They were given to me by my father's friend, Eddie Sinkewich, who was an owner and trainer of Homing Pigeons. Eddie was also a marathon runner; who belonged to the Amesbury A.C. along with my Dad and five other guys. When I first brought them home, I kept them out of doors in a cage up in the apple orchard. I gave them food, water and shelter there to teach them where their new home was located. Fantail Pigeons are a little bit like Homing Pigeons in that, they will wander off for a while, but they always come back home to roost at night.

Homing Pigeons, of course, travel great distances to get back to their coop. When I finally released them, they nested in a nearby pine tree to mate. I left food and water for them out near the barn and kept my eye on their activities. One night, after a couple of months, they did not come home to roost. I looked everywhere, but found no trace of them. I went to Eddie Sinkewich's place, about a half mile away, to see if they may have returned to him. They were not there. His only explanation: they must have been stolen! I could not believe it. Who would steal a pair of pigeons from an 8 year boy? That is when I learned that they where quite valuable.

Here is another hard lesson I had to learn as young lad growing up in Amesbury back in the late 1930's.

One day, I went to answer a knock on our front door and, there, in the doorway was a man, a stranger; holding a cute, small, light brown, puppy dog. The man asked, "Are you Skippy Biron?" I answered, "Yes sir." He handed the puppy to me, who immediately peed all over me; and he said, "This puppy is for you. It comes from your Uncle Albert. He is only a few days old." Then he turned and left me holding this cute little puppy dog in my hands. My Uncle Al was working up in Maine; setting up and breaking down carnival sites for Legasse Amusement Company out of Haverhill. The puppy was one of a litter born to a carnival show dog. Since the dog came from my mother's brother, my Uncle Albert, we named the dog, "Bibs." (Bibs was my uncle's nickname.) In those days, dogs were not allowed in the house except on extremely cold nights in the winter, and even then, they went down into the cellar. My father and I built a dog house out of scrap lumber which we found in the barn. Looking back, I realize now that dog never had a license or any shots either. Bibs was a good dog; he learned to obey simple commands and he followed me everywhere, when I released him from his "run.". We built a long "run" between two trees in the orchard; to which we connected a long leash with a ring. One day, Bibs became very sick and he was diagnosed by my parents in conjunction with our neighbors that he had "distemper" and had to be "put down." There was no veterinarian involved; in fact, a "vet" was not even considered in those days. We could not have afforded one anyway. My father sat me down and explained that because Bibs was my dog; it was my job to "put him down." He ordered me to dig a hole up in the garden and he loaded his double barreled, 12 gauge shotgun with two shells. He showed me how to shoot the shotgun and marched Bibs and I to that hole and said, "Shoot him." I looked at my dog sitting by that hole just looking up at me with those sad eyes; I was hoping that he would run away.

But he did not move; he just sat on the ground beside that hole and stared at me.

I closed my eyes and fired the shotgun. I missed! How could I miss? The muzzle of the shotgun was only inches from the dog's head. Even at the sound of the shotgun blast, Bibs did not move. My father, standing behind me, said, "Don't miss again, I have no more ammunition." I did not miss again. After determining that Bibs was dead, I grabbed the shovel and buried him. To that point in my life, it was the hardest thing I was ever asked to do. Little did I know that life was tough and about to get much tougher. My next dog was a small, black, Labrador Retriever; we called him "Nigger." I don' t remember where we got him, but I do remember that he didn't stay around too long; because he was a "chicken killer."

When that Lab was hooked up to the old "run" we had built for Bibs, he would chase and kill any chickens that came near him. My father was furious; he had too much time and money invested in those chickens. There was an old wives tale that if you hung the dead chicken around the neck of the dog that had killed it, the dog would not kill any more chickens. That is not true. We had a dead chicken hanging around Nigger's neck all the time and he was still chasing the chickens. My father got rid of him and I never asked what he did with him.

In the summers of 1939 and 1940, I attended Camp Tasker, a boy's summer camp located in Newton Junction, NH on Country Pond. The camp was run by the Haverhill Boys Club. I got to go there because the Director of the Boys Club, "Budger" Wysocki and my father had grown up together and were very good friends. In fact, the two men had competed for the director's position and "Budger" got the job. One year, Buddy and I both went to Camp Tasker together. It cost $4.00 per week; 3 meals a day in a dining room setting and we slept at night in bunk houses. There were 6 bunk houses; housing 10 boys and a Councilor.

We learned to swim, hike, canoe, play basketball and horseshoes, sing by a camp fire; we even learned to box. The Councilors were 16-17 year old boys: many of whom were former campers. My Councilor was a great guy whose name was, Leon Deroian. He taught me many things; especially how to swim. Many years later, Leon became Head of the Lifeguards at Salisbury Beach, where he was responsible for saving numerous people from drowning in the Atlantic Ocean.

CHAPTER 4

"School Days"

When I went to school, all the teachers were un-married women, except for my Manual Training teacher, Mr. Ingham. These women were probably just as dedicated to their students as were the nuns at parochial schools. At least, my mother thought so. She did not believe in parochial school education. She just felt, well, it was just too parochial. My favorite teacher was Miss Mary Moran at the Horace Mann School in Amesbury. I had her in both the 2nd Grade and, again in the 4th Grade. Miss Moran had a huge influence on my education. She recommended me for a double promotion in Grade 2, but again, my Mom would have none of it. In fact, I am still in possession of a beautifully bound book entitled, "How People Work Together," which she gave to me "for excellent work in Grade 4." This teacher even took over my religious education when she realized that I was a Catholic boy of 10 or 11 who had never made his First Holy Communion. She proceeded to register me for Sunday School classes so I could make my First Communion that year at Saint Joseph's Church up on Sparhawk Street, about 3 miles from my home.

Grades 1 through 6 (1936-1941), I went to the Horace Mann School in Amesbury. I lived at 82 Congress Street and walked a little over ½ mile to school each day. I started Grade 7 at Amesbury Junior High School on Macy Street, a distance of about 3 miles each way from home. Then, after World War II began, we moved back to Haverhill half way through Grade 7. Grades 7 and 8 (1942-1943), I went to the Tilton Elementary School on Grove Street in Haverhill. We lived at 42 Hancock Street and walked only 2 or 3 blocks to school. Grade 9, Freshman Year was in the High School Annex, through Grade 12 (1945-1948) went to Haverhill High School when it was located on the corner of Summer and Main Streets in Haverhill. The walk from home was 1 ½ miles each way.

I graduated from Haverhill High School in June, 1948. By October, 1948, I was in the U.S. Navy at Great Lakes, IL going to Boot Camp.

An interesting bit of trivia concerning my days at HHS involves the comic strip, "Archie and his Friends." Apparently, the true origin of Archie is Haverhill High School, not Riverdale, which is fictitious. Bob Montana, who created and sketched all the Archie characters; such as, Archie, Betty, Veronica and Jughead, attended Haverhill High a few years before I did. I have learned that many of the characters in the comic strip are based on real people that Montana knew while at HHS. The school librarian in the cartoon, "Miss Grundy", was inspired by Elizabeth Tuck and school principal, "Mr. Weatherbee" was a model of Earl McLeod. They were both still there for the 4 years that I was going to high school. In fact, Earl McLeod's son, Charlie graduated with me in 1948. Archie's Gang hangouts are all based on real locations where I also hung out as a teenager. The Crown Confectionery: "I'll meetcha down the Crown," Tuscarora's on Winter Street: "See ya at Tusky's," and the Chocolate Shop on Merrimack Street.

Many of us Haverhill High School Alumni are still trying to determine which students inspired Bob Montana to create the characters of Archie, Jughead, Veronica and Betty, for example.

CHAPTER 5

"Beautiful, Beautiful Brown Eyes"

On November 2, 1942, my sister, Norma, was born. She was a 6 lb, 8 oz. beautiful, brown eyed, baby girl and everything was right with the world.

Wrong!! The birth of the child went very well, but something had gone radically wrong with my mother, which, even today; nobody knows what happened, why it happened or even when it happened. A day or maybe two later, they discovered, that, either during delivery or shortly after, she had suffered severe brain damage. I remember very clearly, even today, that very early the next morning, November 3rd, she smiled and waved at me from her bedroom window of the Maternity Ward on the second floor of the Amesbury Hospital. The north end of the hospital looked right down on the back side playground of Amesbury Junior High. Everything seemed fine to me then. That night, my father came to me weeping and hugging me saying, "Skippy, Skippy, we are going to lose your Mom. What will we do without her?" He had completely lost it. I had never seen him lose it like that before. At that very moment, I just realized, my time had come. I would have to take over as head of the household because my family was falling apart. I believe that it was the same time I was called by God to help and serve others. I was 12 years old and my service began with my brother and sister and continued for the rest of my life.

Well, my mother did not die; it might have been much better on everyone concerned if she had. In those days, there were very few, if any, mental health facilities or programs available to deal with her situation. No one had Health Insurance, no Blue Cross-Blue Shield, no Medicare and no Medicade. We paid our medical bills on a pay-as-you-go basis out of pocket. The doctors, at the time, were lucky if they got completely paid for your first child while they were delivering your second. Of course, pre-natal and delivery care cost less than $100 in those days and many deliveries were still being done at home. We brought my sister, Norma home from the hospital on schedule, while we were still trying to decide on what to do with my Mom. We talked my Aunt Muriel, my Uncle Bib's wife to come from Portland, ME and live with us and take care of my baby sister for a couple of weeks until Mom could take over. That never happened. Aunt Muriel was a newly wed and she had never taken care of a new-born child before. The first time my Uncle Bibs got a pass from Fort Prebble, where he was stationed, he came to visit us and to see his new bride. I went to see Father Melea at St. Joe's to make the necessary arrangements to get Norma baptized. My Aunt Muriel and my Uncle Bibs agreed to be her Godparents.

That was my first official duty as the unofficial head of the household to be successfully completed. When my mother came home, she was very confused and lethargic. She could not or would not respond to her baby's needs. She was unable to take proper care of herself, let alone a new born child. She was very docile, spoke only when spoken to and seemed to be living in another world. There were occasional break throughs, however. On one occasion, I came into the house bleeding from an injury which I received while playing out of doors. She got up immediately, cleaned, dressed and bandaged that wound like she had done so many times before. She was often gentle and loving with my brother, Buddy. She never forgot that her Buddy was Momma's boy.

After a few weeks, my uncle was begging us to get another care taker for my sister, so his wife could get back to his side. I remember World War II was going full blast. We were living in black-out conditions at night; air raid warning sirens were frequently screaming, there was gas rationing and food stamps. I am describing the living conditions under which we were living to portray an accurate setting for my story. My father was working full time at the hat shop. He had been classified "4F" with the Draft because of his age and family dependency situation, which means he did not have to go into the army. I was going to school every day; I was in the 7th Grade at Amesbury Junior High and Buddy was in the 2nd Grade at the Horace Mann.

We found a young, married couple in West Newbury to take care of Norma on a full time basis for a reasonable fee. I usually visited there once a week, on a Sunday. We bought our first automobile; a 1939 Pontiac Coupe with a long, Indian head for a hood ornament, so that we could visit my sister. I remember that I learned how to drive at 12 along with my Dad because he was a poor driver and he was drinking a lot at the time. On many occasions, I walked up to Johnny's Tavern on Elm Street and drove him home because he was too intoxicated to drive. Once, I had to get him out of a snow drift in which he had managed to get stuck.

It was about this time, we placed Mom in a place called Pearson's Sanatorium because we were told they could help her there. For a very short period of time, the whole situation had reached a plateau of stability. Then, on a cold, winter's night, dressed only in a night gown, robe and slippers, my mother broke out of the sanatorium and walked seven or more miles back home to us on Congress Street. To this day, I do not know how she did that! My father and I mistakenly interpreted that as evidence of a strong desire and determination to return to her family and function as a mother again. We decided to let her stay and did not take her back to the sanatorium. We soon discovered that it was an act of rebellion against the way she was being treated.

Whenever I thought about it later: I wondered, how did she ever find her way home and how did she ever survive the cold?

Everything that we tried only made her worse. Finally, my father was forced to have her committed to the Danvers State Hospital for the mentally ill. It took me many years before I was able to forgive him for committing her; to understand how desperate he must have been and to realize how difficult it must have been for him. The only good news was; my Aunt Elizabeth, my mother's oldest sister worked at the hospital for many years. At least, we had an interested party on the inside to watch over her.

Now my brother and I were constantly being harassed, by both the young and the old with cries of, "Ha, Ha, your Momma's in the nut house!" We managed to overlook their ignorance and malice, but it took a lot of class and guts. My sister, Norma was never exposed to this hypocrisy because of her youth and, besides, she was living apart from us.

It was about this time, we moved back to Haverhill on Hancock Street bringing my sister with us until we could find another nanny for her. I was determined to keep my family together. Besides, the couple who were caring for Norma were becoming too possessive and were pressing us to allow them to adopt her. I transferred Buddy into the 2nd and I went into the 7th grade at the Tilton School on Grove Street, only one street over from Hancock Street.

CHAPTER 6

"Watching Scotty Grow"

Several mental health treatments were being tried on my mother at the state hospital; including the very controversial electric shock treatments. This is a procedure where electrodes are placed at your temples and electricity is transmitted between the electrodes designed to shock your brain back to working correctly. I never understood the reasoning behind this procedure nor did I ever see any favorable results coming from it. I only know that my mother was terrified every time they came near her with those ridiculous electrodes and she begged us to make them stop using them; which they ultimately did. Then I moved my sister in with my Aunt Virginia down on High Street. My Aunt Virginia was either my Uncle Clum's wife or his girl friend; I never knew whether or not they were married and I didn't care. It surely fueled the fires of gossip around town. Family and friends spent more time talking behind our backs than they did helping us out. It is no wonder that I grew up so quickly. I learned two interesting facts during this period in my life; I had not yet reached 14 years of age.

#1—All the insane people are not in the asylums, and
#2—All the people in the asylums are not insane.

By now, as the song goes, I had learned how to cook and to sew, but I don't remember loving it. I had also learned how to iron the pleats on little girl's dresses and how to comb and cut their hair. I did all the grocery shopping and purchased all the clothes for the three of us. Every Friday evening, I met my Dad when he came over the bridge with his pay envelope. He would take a few bucks for himself and give me the rest to run the house. Every school day morning, I would meet "Dumbo" Amaro coming down Hancock Street and we would walk to school together. He was going to trade school, which was on my way to the high school. Each morning without fail, he would ask me for a cigarette; I was smoking cigarettes since I was about 13 years old. Dumbo never had any cigarettes and he was always going to pay me back: never did. He was taking up Auto Repair at the trade school and every time someone would ask him what was wrong with their car whenever it did this or that; Dumbo's usual response: "It could be a lot of things."

Another interesting story about the 5 or 6 years that we lived on Hancock Street. Every Christmas it became incumbent upon me to play Santa Claus for my brother and sister. I did such a good job that my brother continued to believe in Santa Claus until he was 13 or 14 years old.

He was unable to conceive that I was able to purchase, wrap, conceal and ultimately place the gifts under the tree on Christmas Eve without ever being seen. The kids in the neighborhood tried desperately to convince him that I must be performing Santa's Christmas duties, but they were unsuccessful. I was the Tooth Fairy, Easter Bunny and Santa Claus for my younger siblings. It never occurred to me to play it any other way.

One Saturday morning, I responded to a knock on our back door. There in the doorway stood two matronly looking women each with some kind of folder in their hands. I asked them what they wanted and they answered that they would like to come in and look around. "What for?" I asked. Then I realized that these people were from Child Protection Services. One of our nosey neighbors had obviously reported three children living without adult supervision at this address. I invited them in but I was very rude and fresh with them. I gladly showed them our bedrooms with freshly laundered linens and my floors that had all been recently washed and waxed. Our floors were all covered with brightly colored linoleum; no rugs on our floors in those days. Then, my "coup de grace:" I opened my cupboards and "fridge" and showed them all the fresh, nourishing food I had on hand. I told them we were probably eating better than they were and that I was a better cook, as well . Then, I went to the door and told them to leave and never return. They left in a huff and I never saw them again.

Things settled down for about a year or so and then one day, out of the blue, my Mom came home on a trial basis. She settled down to being a wife to my Dad and Mom to Buddy and I. We did not bring my sister, Norma home yet; only for visits on week ends until we were sure that Mom could handle the task. She got about 90% back to her old self.

There were times when she thought she heard voices and thought that the neighbors were taunting her from behind their curtains. I am not sure that it was all imaginary; we did have very nosey and busy-body type of neighbors who did very little to help her through this phase of her recovery.

It was about this time that I got my first real job. I went to work for the Imperial Dye House, the home of City Cleaners on River Street in Haverhill. That cleaning plant served about 10 or 12 stores located all over the Merrimack Valley. I received 40 cents an hour and got about 24 hours of work per week. I helped on the trucks making pick-ups and deliveries between the plant and their store locations. I also worked in the plant marking shirts and helping to load and unload the huge extractors, which is what they called the machines where cleaning of clothes is done. I was earning about $10.00/week; they paid me cash in envelopes. I brought my pay envelope home to my Mom and she would give me $2.00 to spend as I chose and she put the rest away for me for buying school supplies and clothes. Things were humming along pretty well. Then, one day, as I was coming home from work, walking up Hancock Street. I could not help but notice that something was wrong. All our neighbors were very quiet in their yards as I passed by. When I reached our house, I found my Dad home early from work and my brother, Buddy, waiting for me to arrive. What had transpired was very upsetting. One of our busy-body neighbors had been harassing my mother and annoying her from her front room, bay window. So, my Mom marched across the street, picked up a rock and proceeded to throw it right through that large window in front of the house. The neighbors called the cops and they came, picked her up and took her right back to the State Hospital. Her trial period ended just like that: no hearing, no trial, no nothing. Right back to square one. I do not remember her ever coming home again, even when she became well enough to do so. From time to time over the next 2 or 3 years, I did visit her and she surely wanted to come home and try to make it again. Just when it seemed that she had dealt successfully with her mental issues, they discovered that cancer was ravaging her body. In those days, there was no chemotherapy or radiation available to the average person and there were no cancer treatment centers either. They only knew how to do one thing, which I call, "Chop, chop!" The first procedure done on my mother was a double mastectomy; good-bye both breasts. A few months later, they removed both ovaries. My mother was constantly experiencing a high level of pain. She lost a great deal of weight. There was no way that she could be saved. The last time I saw my Mom alive was in 1950 or 1951. I was in the U.S. Navy, home on leave and I called ahead to be sure that she would be able to receive visitors. She welcomed me with open arms, crying out, "Oh, my Skippy, how handsome you are in your sailor suit!" Then, being the eternal mother, she said to me, "Son, you have not been brushing your teeth." She had gone into town and purchased a gift for me. it was a book entitled "Kon Tiki" by Thor Heyerdahl, the Norwegian who proved that the early Polynesians came from South America on large rafts driven by the prevailing winds. I kept that book with me in my sea bag during my entire naval career. By this time, my mother was a frail and tiny person from what she once was. I could see in her eyes that she was in constant pain. Before I left her side, she gave me one of her pearls of wisdom. She asked me if I had a girl friend and when I responded, "Not yet."; she said to me,

"When you meet the right girl, do not let religion come between you." I thought about her parting advice over the years. Needless to say, I never did allow religion to come between me and either of my two wives.

Going back to my childhood days growing up in Amesbury and Haverhill, we had no television; were lucky to have an old Adwater Kent radio with large and very hot vacuum tubes and a long wire antenna which ran around the room. It received only AM radio. It was on this radio that I heard Franklin Delano Roosevelt (FDR) announce that the Japanese had bombed Pearl Harbor on December 7th, 1941. We also had one of those crank-up Victrola record players which played the old 78 RPM vinyl records; monoral, of course. We had no washer or dryer, no telephone; not even a party line. The first television broadcast that I ever saw, was the Ezzard Charles vs. Jersey Joe Walcott fight in 1948. It was broadcast in black and white on a 12 inch, round screen.

We were standing on the sidewalk, looking into the showroom window of Gerson's Furniture Store on Washington Street in Haverhill. The first television set that I ever actually owned was in 1954, when I lived in Salem NH, after I married my first wife. There was no cable TV, so I had to rig my own 5-in-line antenna and strap it to the chimney on the roof. It was a Raytheon 12 inch round, black and white television set which my mother-in-law gave to us because it was not working. So, I had to fix it, of course!

CHAPTER 7

"When You Were Sweet Sixteen"

When I went to school, I was always a good student. I always paid attention in the classroom; never goofed off or fooled around. I took copious notes and never had to cram for exams or tests along the way. I have a fabulous memory; so, I always seemed to know which material we would be tested on. I was always prepared: no surprises. In high school, I made the Honor Roll every semester: all A's and B's. I was enrolled in the College Prep Course; not considered to be a fresh air course! For Math, I took Algebra I and II, Geometry, Trigonometry and Solid Geometry. This course included both Physics and Chemistry, Latin I, II and III; which included translating Caesar and Cicero. Four years of English (required) which included extensive study of both American and English Literature, as well as, Grammar etc. They were able to squeeze Ancient History in there somewhere which was boring. I also took Mechanical Drawing I & II, called Drafting now, as an elective. My modern language choice was Italian I & II which was a piece of cake, having heard Italian spoken in the home as a child. I aspired to be a Lawyer; what happened? I passed my College Boards and applied to Harvard Law School. There were no scholarships, no student loans in those days and no parental support. The Draft Board was on my back: I was classified "1A."

During my Senior Year in high school, I went to work at the Haverhill Shoe Novelty Co. on Essex Street in Haverhill on an early release program from school. That meant that I left school early each school day at 12:00 noon instead of the normal 1:30 PM. I was working from 1:00 to 4:00 PM and sometimes on Saturday mornings, as well. We were manufacturing buttons and bows for ladies shoes and also brass studded ribbon that was to be cemented around the edges of platform shoes. In the Sophomore and Junior years in high school, I delivered the Haverhill Gazette, the local newspaper, to 154 customers on a daily basis, Monday through Saturday. I used to make my collections on Sundays after Mass. My customers were usually home on Sunday morning and the tips were better then. The paper route actually belonged to Joe Balter, a member of our Currier Square gang, but he wanted to play high school sports and the practices occurred after school when he was usually delivering the Gazette. He actually paid me more than he was clearing on the route, so he finally gave the paper route to me. The bulk of the route, 86 customers; was located on 2 streets; Pilling and Hancock. I delivered to every tenant in all the triple deckers and two family homes on those streets. I paid Abie Lawrence $2.00 a week just to deliver the papers on those two streets.

He couldn't make any mistakes; he delivered the same paper to every house. I collected on Sunday and got all the tips, as well; Abie got $2.00 a week period. Looking back, I was a pretty good business man then. I delivered the front end of the route myself after picking up my papers at the Gazette Office located behind the Colonial Theater on Essex Street, count off 86 papers, tie them in a bundle and put the bundle on the Mt. Washington bus. The bus driver would kick the bundle off the bus at Currier Square in front of Arthur Peever's drug store, where Abie would pick them up. After picking up the bundle of papers, he would go around the corner on to Pilling Street, deliver the Gazettes on both sides of the street, turn right on Boston Street and right again on Hancock and deliver both sides of that street and he was done; less than 30 minutes in good weather. Very convenient because both Abie and I lived on Hancock Street. At the beginning of the route, I walked across Washington Square; left 6 papers in the lobby of the Hotel Whittier, 4 papers at Norma's Beauty Salon a few doors up the street, 2 papers at the Roma Café & the Lithuanian Tavern, a paper at the White Eagle Market (where I bought our groceries on a tab), and 2 papers at the Polish National Home. I delivered the

Haverhill Gazette to most of the businesses between Washington Square and Currier Square. The end of my portion of the route was on Porter, Baldwin, Sheppard Streets and the Currier Tavern, which are located around the periphery of the square.

In the late 1940's, I was a teenager growing up in Haverhill, I hung out with a gang of young fellows who lived in the neighborhood. World War II had just ended and many of the older brothers of my friends never came home. Most of us were in jeopardy of being drafted into the U.S. Army. I was classified "1A" and was eligible to be "called up" upon graduation from high school. We met and congregated on the park benches located in Currier Square by the old horse watering trough. The park benches were our meeting place and hangout. We lived in the area around the square on Grove, Hancock, Pilling, High, Bartlett, Sheppard and Porter Streets. We never locked our doors and we never sat for hours staring at a "boob tube" because there was no television. No one in the gang owned an automobile. We walked everywhere and on occasion, we took the bus. If one us was able to borrow our Dad's car, we all pitched in for gas and headed for Revere Beach or Salisbury Beach looking for girls. We always returned the car with empty ash trays and a full tank of gas. Gas was only 20-25 cents a gallon. Although we never called him that, we invented the "designated driver" because we never allowed our driver to drink alcoholic beverages when we were carousing to ensure our own safety and make sure their Daddy's car got back home in one piece.

Although most of us were of Italian descent, there were guys of Irish, Polish, French and Jewish origins; plus one black kid (called African Americans now?), whose name was Donald Shaw, but we called him "Jackie" in honor of Jackie Robinson who was breaking into the major leagues with the Brooklyn Dodgers at the time. We did not call our black or negro friends "African-American" in those days; and, we did not call ourselves "Italian-American" either. We were all simply "American" period. The most significant thing here is that we all got along very well with each other in a very cosmopolitan environment and never got in trouble with the law. Across the

Merrimack River in Bradford, there was a gang of girls who hung out at the Fruit Basket in Central Square.

Some of them went to high school with me at Haverhill High. Four or five of these Bradford Girls "went steady" with guys in our Currier Square Gang. Both groups would socialize at various events; such as, school dances, football and basketball games. I was very proud and honored to be associated with this bunch of young men. We did everything together. When we went to the movies at the Paramount Theater on Main Street, we would sometimes occupy two complete rows of seats in the balcony. High school graduations were held in the Paramount Theater in the 1940's. The graduating class would march from the high school on Summer Street, three blocks down Main Street to the theater, where the graduating exercises were held.

We formed a singing group that sang in the evenings on the park benches. We would harmonize in a kind of barber shop quartet style doing songs like "Up a Lazy River" and "Paper Doll." We had a guy, "Haunt" Scorsoni, who could imitate musical instrument sounds vocally like the Mills Brothers used to do back in the 30's and 40's. We were pretty good and passers by would stop and listen. Frank Sinatra was just becoming popular in the music world. The "Zoot Suit" was the style, with the wide brimmed hat, pegged pants, long watch chain and pointed toed shoes. I remember that my pants were so small at the cuff that I had to remove my shoes to put my pants on or take them off. One of my friends, Corrado Marino, went all the way with the zoot suit style, especially when he came to school. He and Sonny Alonzi were the two wildest zoot suiters in the city of Haverhill.

Late on hot summer nights, neighbors could hear the loud sounds of us playing "Tutta La Morta", an Italian finger game. People yelled out in the night, "Vatina la casa!" (Translation--Go home!)

When I came down Hancock Street heading for Currier Square, some of the Italian women who were always gossiping over the fence, would call out and say, "Hey, boy, you worka? Gooda boy! You no worka? Badda boy!" Nobody ever thought that any good would ever come from the members of our gang.

We had enough bodies and talent around the neighborhood to form the nucleus of a very competitive basketball team which competed in the Haverhill YMCA Junior League for a few years. We located a coach and sponsor who supplied our uniforms and we even won the city championship a couple of seasons. In the summer, we formed a baseball team from the neighborhood and competed in a City Junior League, which played at a level similar to Junior Legion Baseball. We had a very competitive bunch of guys who hung out together, played hard and clean and made a good accounting of ourselves.

We called ourselves the Capo Gang, short for Capoville. The origin of the Capoville team name was conceived by Ty Abate, who came up with the idea as a way to honor our very first sponsor; a local, Italian merchant whose last name was Capodelupo. (Means--Head of the Wolf)

Our basketball team became known as the Capoville Nationals and the baseball team was the Capoville Comets. We even had a football team for a short period of time called the Capoville Bears; who were undefeated in the first season. Someone got seriously injured on another team because of inadequate protective equipment and the league was disbanded.

My father, Diddy Biron, coached all of these teams for many years. He was able to achieve success with kids who had only average talent. He would use his wit coupled with experience and knowledge of the game to produce a winning team. I will always remember the following situation which actually occurred in a baseball game many years ago. It was late in the game and the opposing pitcher had not given up many hits. There was a runner on third base representing the winning run and there were 2 outs. The batter at the plate was not one of the best hitters on the team. My Dad was coaching 3rd base. The ball was in play; time out had not been called. Just as the opposing pitcher was about to deliver a pitch to the plate, my father, standing in the 3rd base coaching box, called to the pitcher, "Hey, Son, Let me take a look at that ball!"

The kid stepped off the rubber, without thinking, threw the ball to my Dad in the coaches box; who stepped aside allowing the ball to go into foul territory. Then the runner on third base was directed to go home and score the winning run. It was a very controversial call, but legal! People talked about that play for years after.

Here is another example to illustrate our ability to be successful with just a bunch of average kids that hung around the corner. When we were just beginning to form our baseball team, we found ourselves in need of a second baseman. All the positions were filled except 2nd base. The only guy remaining without a slot on the team was, Joe Venezia. But Joe was a southpaw, a left hander. In those days, no one ever heard of a leftie playing 2nd base because it is so difficult for them to execute a double play. My father, the eternal coach, spent hours teaching Joe how to pivot in the opposite direction, clockwise toward center field, then come over the top and throw left handed to first base. It wasn't very long before Joe was able to successfully complete a double play. My father told us that he learned that technique when he was a young man, barnstorming around the country with the old House of David baseball team from Haverhill.

House of David baseball was played by a group of men, who were not necessarily Jewish, but required to grow beards. They were noted for their tremendous ball handling and exceptionally long beards.

By the way, we also had a left handed catcher behind the plate; a fellow named, Charlie Penta. Because we were unable to find a left handed catcher's mitt for him; Charlie learned to play with a right handed mitt on the opposite hand. He simply placed his thumb where the little finger belonged and vice versa. Charlie was a damn good catcher, too. We had to keep our eye on Charlie because he suffered from Rheumatic Fever.

CHAPTER 8

"Anchors Aweigh"

In the summer of 1948, the Capoville Gang rented a cottage at Salisbury Beach for 2 weeks. It was actually a Quonset Hut; it's not there any more, there are condominiums on that site now. During our vacation at the beach, Dick O'Neal and I decided to join the U.S. Navy. We sat on the beach one day and looked out over the Atlantic Ocean wondering what lie out there and decided to find out. We actually joined under the "buddy system," which turned out to be a joke! We didn't even arrive at Boot Camp together. I was in Company #386 and he was in Company #382. My company was located in Camp Porter and his was in Camp Downes at Great Lakes. One night just before taps was sounded, I heard a voice in the night, calling, "Skippy Biron, are you here? Can you hear me?" It was my buddy,

Dick O'Neal roaming among the barracks trying to find me by calling out my name. It worked! That's how we finally got together at Great Lakes Naval Training Center. I went on to Radio School in Norfolk, VA. when we left boot camp and Dick went aboard the USS Robert H. McCard DD822 tied up in Newport, RI. He served his entire enlistment as an engineman on that destroyer. We hooked up only one more time before we were discharged. My ship, the USS Kearsarge CV33, was in dry dock in South Boston Navy Yard. One afternoon, while I was up on the flying bridge, I spotted a tincan with "822" painted on the bow, steaming into Boston Harbor, heading for Charlestown Navy Yard across the bay. I raised the McCard on flashing light from the bridge and arranged to meet Dick at the YMCA in City Square located right outside the navy yard gate in Charlestown. We met, shot some pool and caught up on old times. I never saw him again until many years later when we were both back in civilian life. When I enlisted in the Navy, I was able to choose the service school I was to attend after boot camp because I received such a high score on my General Classification Test (GCT) before I was even sworn in. I chose Radio School because the course was only 16 weeks in Norfolk, VA and I went to sea. In October, 1948, I was sworn into the U.S. Navy in the old Custom House Building in downtown Boston. The first thing I learned there was that I was not the only Edward Biron being sworn in that day. When we mustered for the ceremony, two Edward Birons toed the line; Edward A. Biron from Manchester, NH and Edward J. Biron from Haverhill, MA and we ended up in the same company at boot camp. After we left boot camp, we went separate ways but that did not prevent us from receiving each other's mail for many years after. Our group went from South Station in Boston by train via the water-level-route all the way to Great Lakes, IL It was a troop carrier; no sleepers, but there was a dining car to be used at our own expense. I played lots of poker on that train, made a few bucks; but got hardly any sleep on those hard seats.

After we received our sea bag and our clothing issue; next came the short haircut and all the required shots. Boot camp was a great experience for me. I learned to march in formation, marlinespike and seamanship. I went to fire fighting school and gunnery school. I loved every bit of it; just ate it up. I took my first 6 hour liberty and went to Waukegan; where Jack Benny was born. We graduated just before Christmas and everyone went home again via troop trains to our various parts of the country for Christmas and New Years leave. We returned to Great Lakes in early January, 1949.

A few days later, I was on a train heading for the naval service schools in Norfolk, VA. I started attending the Radio Operator's School just a couple of days after I arrived there. I was impressed; everything seemed so well coordinated. Right away, I learned to send and receive International Morse Code with a telegraphic key. At first, we copied the code with a stick (pencil). Then, as our speed increased, we had to use a typewriter to keep up. We learned to type on a "Telegraphic Mill" which had no shift key; everything was upper case. No punctuation. We used the letter "x" for a period, comma, question mark etc. For those who can remember, this is the way that Western Union Telegrams used to look. By the time I left radio school, I could send and receive between 20 and 30 words per minute, and, of course, I had to be able to type 30 words per minute. We also learned how to tune up the transmitters and receivers that we may soon encounter aboard ship. I got a some Teletype Training there, as well. Teletypewriter Technology was just beginning to be used aboard ship at this particular time. Radio School, like many service schools, operated on two week increments. If a student passed the first two weeks of the program, then he moved on to the next two week increment and so forth. If you failed any two week requirement, you had to repeat it with the next class coming along behind yours. A new class started every two weeks. If you repeated any two week increment too many times, you washed out and were forced to join the fleet as a deck hand where you chipped paint, handled lines or worked on the Mess Decks. Not a very happy future, I'm afraid.

Bob DePaoli and I, along with about 40 other men and women (there were WAVES in Radio School), graduated and moved on in early May, 1949. Bob and I went to Quonset Point, R.I. where we became Radiomen for the Admiral, who was Commander Fleet Air Wing 15 and whose flag was flying aboard the USS Kearsarge CV-33. Well, the Admiral moved on without us and we became part of ship's company. We were tied up on one side of a large pier and the USS Oriskany CV-34 was tied up on the other side. Both were Essex Class Aircraft Carriers; the last two of that class to be commissioned during World War II. Both were built in the Brooklyn Navy Yard. The Kearsarge had about sixty Radiomen aboard to handle 6 radio shacks and 1 Communication Center. We had a large number of whip type antennas located fore and aft on the starboard side which had to raised and lowered every time the aircraft were launched or recovered. My battle station was Radio 7, which was located aft on the starboard side right under the flight deck. I was responsible for lowering these antenna when aircraft were active on the flight deck and bringing them back up to their normal operating position by using a hand operated crank and counter balance setup. The huge compressors that operate the cables to which the landing hook mounted on each plane had to capture upon landing, were located right over Radio 7 and made a terrible racket. If a plane lost it's hook or if the hook failed to capture the cable, the plane would go over the side into the sea. At first, the Navy used tin-cans (destroyers) as plane guards. Later, choppers (helicopters) were used as plane guards to pluck the planes from the sea.

In May, 1949, the USS Kearsarge was anchored off-shore at Port-au-Prince, Haiti, where Dumarsais Estime was the leader. There was a lot of political unrest because of a corrupt government and mis-appropriation of funds that came from all over the world to help prevent disease resulting from an earthquake there. Everyone wanted to know, "Where did the money go?" There was an aerial photograph of the CV-33 riding the hooks (anchors) with the entire crew manning the rail in dress whites published in every major newspaper in the world. With a copy of that photo in hand, I am able to show viewers exactly where I was standing on that day.

In August 1949, the Kearsarge was part of a Navy Week celebration in Halifax, Nova Scotia. Ships from the United States, United Kingdom and Canada took part. Another aircraft carrier, USS Midway CVB-41 also participated. Later that same year, the Kearsarge spent 6 months in drydock at the South Boston Shipyard at the Army Base. It was during this particular time that I met the girl who was to become my first wife. From Boston Navy Yard, I took many weekend liberties in the Lawrence-Methuen area and that was how we first met.

While operating on the Atlantic Coast, we made a couple of visits to Cuba; we were forced to go to Guantanamo Bay, which the U.S. sailors called "Gitmo." We were limited to base liberty there because Havana was off-limits for the mysterious sinking of the battleship, USS Maine in Havana harbor in 1898. "Remember the Maine!" The United States has occupied the base at Quantanamo under various leases since then. The 45 Sq. Mi. tract is located on the southeastern tip of Cuba and has been used as a naval base, refugee camp and detention center. It may have served all those purposes well over the years, but it was a lousy liberty port and most of the sailors remained aboard ship when tied up there. The Kearsarge operated along the Atlantic Coast and the Caribbean until January, 1950.

When the Korean War began, the CV-33 found itself unable to handle jet planes because it still had a wooden (Douglas Fir) flight deck. We were ordered to the Puget Sound Naval Shipyard in Bremerton, WA to be de-commissioned and obtain a new, steel flight deck enabling the handling of jet planes. The Kearsarge arrived in Bremerton in February 1950. The journey required transiting the Panama Canal. It became the largest ship to ever pass through the canal up to that time. The task required that certain guns and other projecting items near the water line had to be cut away from the hull with acetylene torches; placed carefully on the flight deck and restored later. This procedure made the ship's hull narrow enough to get through the locks. The flight deck overhung the caisson so much, the water level had to be critically controlled when pumping the water level up and down while going in and out of each lock. Still, the underside of the flight deck cut the corrugated metal roof off the pumping station at the Gatun Locks.

The passage took about six or seven hours and when we arrived on the Pacific side of the canal, we tied up to a dock to restore the vessel to a more seaworthy condition for sailing on to Puget Sound. I was able to obtain liberty and go into Panama City that night until midnight; no overnight liberty was being granted in Panama in those days. The U.S. Canal Zone was 5 miles wide on each side of the canal running right through the Republic of Panama. The canal was not nationalized to Panama until 1979 under President Jimmy Carter. The liberty pass afforded me the opportunity to look up a member of our old Currier Square Gang, Jimmy (The Haunt) Scorsoni. We called him, Haunt because he was always around and always in the way. I knew that he was stationed at Albrook AFB there in the U.S. Canal Zone and that he was a musician playing with the Air Force Band stationed there. He played the clarinet and saxophone since he was a youngster in grammar school and went on to play for Haverhill High School marching band and orchestra. I had hooked up with him earlier in our military careers when I was in U.S. Navy Radio School in Norfolk, Va. and he was with an U.S. Air Force Band located in Washington, D.C. From the dock to which we were tied up, I called the air base on the telephone and spoke to the Officer of the Day (OD) who informed me that he was not on the base; he had gone to town. He went on further to tell me where I might find him in Panama City, indicating that it was a long shot. I told the OD that I only had a few hours; we were sailing in the morning. He gave me directions to a bar, a real dive, in the inner city which had become a hangout for musicians, bandsmen and, of course, druggies. With the help of a local taxi driver and few American dollars, I found the place and the "Haunt." He was wearing civilian clothes and I recognized him immediately. After a few beers, he introduced me to a soldier from the Mt. Washington section of Haverhill by the name of Al Poro. He was with the U.S. Army Coast Artillery stationed there in the Canal Zone. He and I were the only two people in uniform in the entire place. We had a little reunion right there in a "dive" in beautiful, downtown Panama City; three guys from Haverhill, Mass; a sailor, a soldier and an airman.

I never saw Haunt Scorsoni again. I heard he passed away shortly after he got home from the service. The CV-33 sailed north at 0700 the next morning.

I stayed around with most of the crew, living in APL's (barracks boats) tied up along side the dock for the first couple of months assisting with the de-commissioning process.

In June of 1950, Stan Peak from Dayton, OH, Larry Graffam from Old Town, ME, Bob DePaoli and I left Bremerton and headed for Treasure Island Navy Base in San Francisco, CA for a new assignment. All of us were radiomen on the Kearsarge looking for another job. We took a 2 week re-location leave and drove from state of Washington to California along the coastal route. Stan had purchased an old 1939 Plymouth Sedan and the rest of us shared the expenses to make the trip. We stopped and did some sight seeing along the way. Our itinerary included a day in Portland, OR and Crescent City, CA. We drove through the huge redwood trees and spent time in Sacramento, CA. One night we had a great time in a VFW Lodge in Redwood City, CA. Our trip took us to 3 state capitols: Olympia, WA, Salem, OR and Sacrament, CA.

When we finally turned ourselves in at Treasure Island, Stan sold the old '39 Plymouth which had served us well. We spent only a few days at T.I. and Bob and I went off on a new assignment to Adak, Alaska by way of Elmendorf Air Force Base in Anchorage and Navy Air Base in Kodiak. Alaska. I never did find out where Stan and Larry ended up.

When landing for the first time at Adak, we had a very traumatic experience. It seems the plane overshot the runway by a half mile and the pilot had to literally stand the plane on it's tail, almost stalling out to avoid running into the mountain at the end of the runway. We came around and made another approach and landed safely. The plane was an old, military C47, propeller driven aircraft with an enlisted man (CPO) at the controls. Those C47's made a lot of noise and vibrated like crazy. That is how we managed to get from place to place back then. I spent about 18 months in the Aleutian Islands, 8 of which was on Attu. I was promoted to Radioman 3rd Class (RM3) while serving on Attu. I had taken the test for RM3 on Adak before I ever hit Attu. There was very little to do on Adak after working your shift at the radio shack, which stood in the middle of a large antenna farm about a half mile from the barracks. I played poker, went drinking at the NCO Club and went to the movies. I also played chess on both Adak and Attu. I ran into a couple of real good chess players there and was able to sharpen my skills.

One evening, there was a lot of excitement on my watch. I picked up a distress call (SOS) on 500 Khz, the International calling frequency for distress at sea. I took control of the situation because it was a very strong signal. It came from a Japanese freighter, the Kimikara Maru with a cargo of iron ore bound for Seattle from Yokosuka, Japan. Their call was "JCIN" and they were transmitting from a "spark-gap" radio transmitter judging from the chirping sound of their signal. I sent one of my crew to the roof for an RDF (radio direction finder) bearing on the vessel in trouble. The message from the Japanese vessel was, "Ship taking water, no steerage, no weigh on, need help!" All of the communication with the distressed vessel was being monitored by other ships and shore stations up and down the Aleutian Chain.

The Commandant of the Seventeenth Naval District (COM17) on Kodiak relieved me of control after I obtained the data necessary to implement a rescue. I continued to standby in case there was further need for our services. COM17 dispatched a Coast Guard cutter at Ocean Station "Sugar," a weather station at sea, which was nearby. They also sent a plane with pumps and rafts from 10th Rescue, an Air Force unit from Adak to assist in the rescue. A few days later, the Kimikara Maru was towed into Adak where repairs were made. The Japanese skipper came out to the radio shack to thank us for our help. We also received a commendation from COM17. While on Attu, another exciting event took place worth reporting here.

Word came down the chain, that Bob Hope was going to do a show on Shemya, an island about 35 miles away from Attu. The show was either going to or returning from Korea and if the guys on Attu could get there on their own, we would be welcome to attend. The USS Bagaduce, ATA-194, a sea-going tugboat was on the dock at Attu at the time. I convinced the skipper to make the trip, but I had to convince my skipper to reduce our detachment to a skeleton crew for a few hours, so the rest of the crew could go over to Shemya to see the show. I got to go after making a few maneuvers with the personnel involved. The show was held in a large hangar at the Air Force Base on Shemya. Beside Bob Hope, the Hollywood blond bombshell, Marilyn Maxwell and the country singer, Jimmy Wakely were in the show. After the show, we headed right back to Attu at full speed. The entire excursion took about 8 or 9 hours. We pulled it off without a hitch!

When my tour was up on Adak, I had to get back to the states, report into the San Diego Naval Base, get leave papers cut so I could get home for Christmas and New Years. The trick was to get transportation to the states. Military air was very limited and there was no commercial air available. The USS Namakagon AOG-53, a Patapsco-Class tanker, was unloading at the Fuel Depot on Adak and preparing to return to San Pedro, CA to pick up another load of fuel before Christmas. Being a radioman in these cases is a big advantage because they know all about the movement of ships and planes in the area. I went aboard the Namakagon requesting passage to San Pedro and offered to stand watch as the ship's Radioman enroute. My offer was accepted, I got my transfer papers endorsed, grabbed my sea bag and boarded the Namakagon. We set sail for the states that night. The seas were high and the ride was rough; an empty tanker rides high and bumpy. They had to take on sea water as ballast to smooth out the ride and prevent splitting some seams.

When the ship docked in San Pedro, I grabbed a taxi cab with my seabag and went over the bridge to the Long Beach Greyhound bus terminal, where I caught the next bus to San Diego. I reported in at the Naval Base, checked my sea bag and found an empty rack to sleep on in the transient quarters. The next morning, I had my leave papers endorsed for 21 days and I was to report back there for my next assignment. Using both military and civilian transportation, I got back to Methuen, MA and stayed with my Aunt Jeannie and Uncle John at 5 Arnold Street.

I spent Christmas with them, visiting my family and friends in the area. I took one of my old girl friends, Rosie Feoli from Lawrence out on a date to Conn's Melody Lounge on Essex Street in Lawrence. Upon entering the establishment, I spotted my Memiere Biron sitting on a bar stool with her "boy friend," who was a barber from Methuen. They were both at least in their seventies. I went over to say, "Hello" to my grandmother and chat for a moment. When I returned to my date, she asked me, "Who is that lady?" and I said, "That's my grandmother." She did not believe me, and said, "See the guy she's with, he's my grandfather." My Memiere Biron was still a fine looking woman. She dyed her hair blond, wore high heels and very stylish clothes. Her middle name was Filomena; we had long ago began calling her "Filly."

A few days before New Years eve, I hopped on a train to Brooklyn to visit Bill Spurge, my old Navy friend. He was no longer in the service, having received a dependency discharge to care for his widowed mother. I was about to fulfill a lifelong dream: to spend New Years eve in Times Square; to watch the ball come down at midnight with all the drama associated with the event. My dream came true on January 1st 1952. Bill and I were there in the center of all the bedlam. I never was kissed so much in all my life. We had a great time that night!

A couple of days later, I took the James Witcomb Riley, an over night train between Grand Central Station and Union Station in Cincinnati. I had learned through the "grapevine" that my friend, Bob DePaoli, had successfully left Adak shortly after I did and made it home for Christmas, as well. My plan was to hook up with Bob in

Cincy, visit for a few days and return to San Diego together. That's exactly what we did. I met Bob's parents and friends. We went on a double date over the L&N Bridge to Covington, KY, which in those days, was a little "sin city." I finally met the girl who had been writing pen pal letters to me all the time I was in the Aleutian Islands. Her name was, Jo Preston, and she lived at the YWCA in Cincy with Mae Wycoff, Bob's lady friend. It turned out that she was much taller than I, making it very clumsy to dance with her or even kiss her, unless we were sitting down. I never saw her again and we exchanged letters only for a short while after that. Bob and I traveled from Cincinnati to San Diego together by way of Chicago. Soon after arriving in San Diego, I was assigned to the USS Bellatrix AKA-3, which was docked in San Pedro. The AKA-3 was an Arcturus Class attack cargo ship and it was named after that star in the constellation Orion. Bob reported aboard the USS Ruddy Am-380, which was an Auk Class minesweeper lying at anchor right there in San Diego. I did not see Bob Depaoli again until 50 years later under very unusual circumstances.

At this point, I must digress and go back to that October, 1948, morning when I left Haverhill for Boston to be sworn into the U.S. Navy. We were all living on High Street in Haverhill at my Aunt Virginia's place. That morning, when I awoke to leave for Boston, my brother said "goodbye" to me.

We had been sleeping in the same bed since he outgrew his crib. Anyway, we said our goodbyes and I did not see him or even know where he was for 12 years. My Aunt Virginia woke up also to see me off. I remember that she gave me $8.00 in cash because she knew I had no money. I increased that little stash to about $20.00 by playing poker on the train from Boston to Great Lakes, which kept me in cigarettes and spending money until I received my first pay in the Navy.

At some point, I have no idea when, while I was away in the service, my father took my sister, Norma and gave her to his sister, my Aunt Jeannie who lived on Arnold Street in Methuen, to care for her indefinitely. My Aunt Jean and Uncle John must have been delighted because they had no children of their own and had been considering adoption. At the same time, my father and brother left Haverhill permanently and moved to Methuen. They moved into a rooming house on Broadway in Methuen, called Ryan's Manor, just a few blocks from my Aunt Jean's house. I learned much later that Buddy was going to school at the Edward F. Searles High School in Methuen and my father was working in the Pacific Mills in Lawrence, where his brother, my Uncle Tom, was an overseer. I have no idea when this all happened or how long the situation existed. I found out long after these events occurred. The next time I heard anything concerning my father, brother or sister, was a year later. I heard that my father had taken my sister, Norma for a normal visit from my Aunt Jean's house and under the cover of darkness moved himself, my brother and maybe my sister and drove off to only God knows where. They all disappeared from the face of the earth. It was two or three days before anyone even were sure that they had left town. When I found out, I was very upset because this meant that he also had abandoned my Mom who was still languishing in the hospital suffering with terminal cancer. I came home on an emergency leave for a few days to help locate them. That is how I learned of the foregoing information. I was unable to help out. I found out many years later that, only my Uncle Tom and Aunt Kay knew where they were; they were sworn to secrecy. They were living on Center Street, right around the corner from Ryan's Manor. I suspected all along that knew where my father and siblings were, but they just kept on denying it.

Back to San Pedro and the USS Bellatrix. We were training off the California coast, preparing to return to Korea. Some of the exercises included lowering our Mike Boats (LCM's) to the rail, setting them into the water while still under weigh; then, circling them up and heading them toward the beach for an assault. There were 6 LCM's aboard; 3 on the starboard and 3 on the port side.

This procedure had to be performed quickly and safely so as not to present a good target for enemy shore batteries and to add an element of surprise. One night, the Skipper had me wakened and called me to the bridge to inform me that my Mom had passed away. He told me if I wanted to go home for the funeral, arrangements could be made. Next morning, a chopper took me ashore, where I picked up some cash from Navy relief and headed home for my Mother's funeral. The first leg out, I caught a military hop from Moffet Field near Sacramento to Kansas City. Sitting beside me on the flight, was a well decorated U.S. Marine. He had a musicians insignia on his sleeve indicating that he must be a member of a Marine Corp band detachment. He kept looking at me and I at him thinking, I know this guy from somewhere. He was obviously thinking the same thing. Then, out of the blue, he looked at me and said, "You're Skippy Biron." At the very same moment, I looked back and said, "Philip Miller!" Yes, we surely knew each other. We went to school together at the Horace Mann School in Amesbury; Grades 1 through 6. He played the Cornet in school, which accounts for the bandsman insignia on his sleeve; he was obviously still playing. We had not seen each other in 10 years from 1942 to 1952. Neither one of us had really changed that much, except for having grown up and maturing in a very complicated world. He told me that when the Korean War broke out, he was in Japan playing in the Marine Corp marching band there. He was, along with other bandsmen, conscripted to become a stretcher bearer on the front lines in Korea. He had to carry the seriously wounded soldiers back to the nearest field medical unit for critical care. Judging from the medals and citations that he wore on his chest, he must have been responsible for saving many lives. We did not talk very much about that, but we did talk about going home and what it was like when we went to grammar school together more than 10 years earlier. We arrived at Westover Field near Springfield, MA together after catching a couple more military hops. We parted company there. He went on to Amesbury and I called my Uncle Tony and Aunt Jenny who lived in Hadley, MA. They came, picked me up and drove me to my Aunt Jean's in Methuen. Unfortunately, my mother had already been buried in Linwood Cemetery in Haverhill earlier on the same day that I arrived. I had suffered very severe ear aches from flying in those WWII (C47's & C54's) airplanes. Those planes were not very well pressurized, besides being very rough riding even in mild turbulence. That night, my Aunt Jean called her doctor who came out on a Saturday night with everything he needed in his satchel. He had the ear drops and antibiotics required; never even wrote a prescription.

Thank God, doctors were still making house calls in 1952. Because I was a serviceman, he never even charged us for the house call. Things have certainly changed. The next morning, I was good to go and never got ear aches from flying again.

I got back to the West Coast and the Bellatrix almost the same way that I had come east, except I did not need a chopper to get aboard. My ship was tied up at a dock in San Pedro. While serving on the Bellatrix, I became very good friends with a sailor from Worcester, MA. He was a Signalman and he had a great "handlebars" mustache. His name was Romeo Duval and he was a good chess player. Romeo and I devised an ingenious method to play chess when we were on watch aboard ship. I would set up a chess board on a chair in the radio shack beside my normal position. Romeo would set one atop the flag bag up on the signal bridge. Using the "voice tube" which ran from the bridge to the radio shack, we would exchange our moves. This worked well because the voice tube did not interfere with any other circuit or operation on the ship. It became our own private line of communication.

One day, I left the hatch open, that connected the shack to the inboard companion way. Suddenly, I got that feeling that one gets when you sense that someone is standing behind you. There, standing in the open hatch, was the skipper of the ship; a full 4 stripe Captain, equivalent to a full bird Colonel in the U.S. Army or Air Force. I came immediately to attention. The Captain steps in and says, "At ease, Sparky." I returned to my seat anticipating a reprimand of some kind. He asked me who I was playing chess with and I responded, "Signalman Duval, up on the signal bridge, Sir." He proceeded to ask me if Romeo was any good at chess and some other small talk. He told me about how he and his wife played chess a lot when they were stationed on Guam during WWII. He asked me if I would come to his stateroom sometime to play chess with him. I said that I would and he left. Whew, I thought, I didn't expect to get off that easy. Just when I had forgotten about the incident, the Captain's Marine Orderly comes below to the crew's quarters one evening looking for Radioman Biron. He told me that the skipper requested my presence in his quarters to play chess. I remember that I won the first game that we played; I think he underestimated me. After that, I was lucky if I won one out of every three or four games. I did, however get to sample his choice wines and enjoy his fancy stateroom. When the Bellatrix was ready to return to Korea, I was transferred to the USS Polk County, LST-1084 which was anchored off 28th Street Landing in San Diego. My one year extension of my original enlistment was due to expire.

When my original tour had expired, almost one year earlier, I was offered a couple of choices; re-enlist for 4 or 6 more years and get promoted to Radioman 2nd Class (RM2), I had already passed the test and was on a waiting list; or accept a one year extension. Throughout the Armed Forces, the one year extension was called Harry Truman's Year. I did not re-enlist, in spite of the monetary incentives the Navy was offering to people holding a critical rate. Radiomen were always on the critical list because they are hard to train and there are never enough experienced high speed operators around. They were offering $300 for every year already served and $300 for every year that one re-enlisted. It was very tempting to a lot of servicemen, especially those who had already served a couple of hitches. It would have been worth $3000 for me if I re-enlisted for 6 years; a lot of money at the time. But, I turned it down and I was never sorry about it.

The LST-1084 was "nested" with 3 other LST's between 2 buoys called a mooring. The watch duty was shared by all four boats at the same mooring. This meant I had the radio watch duty for all 4 LST's every 4th day. I was running back and forth from San Diego and Long Beach almost on a daily basis. When I was aboard the Bellatrix in San Pedro, I met a girl, Mary, who lived right off the "Pike" in Long Beach. I spent all of my liberties with her. She was a sales person working on a salary plus commission basis in a furniture store in Long Beach which specialized in expensive brands of home furnishings.

She entertained thoughts of us marrying one day. I did not share the same thoughts. I was not yet ready to marry; I was enjoying myself too much. Someone once said, "Why buy the cow when milk is so cheap?" I remember one night that we spent together when a strong earth quake woke us up. She got out of bed and began getting dressed. When I asked her what she was doing, she said, "I don't want to be found dead without any clothes." I rest my case. Not too bright. She was very good to me though. She bought me a nice, leather jacket, slacks, loafers and colorful shirts so that we could hang out looking like an ordinary civilian couple. I wore my uniform only when going back and forth to the ship. Shortly after that episode, the LST-1084 went back to Korea and I was transferred again. This time to the Naval Base where I did Shore Patrol (SP) duty in downtown San Diego until I was discharged from the Navy.

CHAPTER 9

"Get Your Kicks on Route 66"

When the final day came, September 18, 1952, I packed my sea bag and shipped it to my Aunt Jean's house in Methuen via Railway Express. I stuffed some toilet articles and a few changes of socks and underwear into a duffle bag and hitchhiked to Long Beach to say goodbye to Mary.

In a few days, on a Sunday evening, at sundown, Mary drove me, with reluctance to Pasadena to the beginning (or ending) of Route 66, where I began my journey home. I decided to hitchhike home by way of Route 66. Like the song says, I was going to "get my kicks on Route 66!"; another one of my lifetime dreams. I arrived in Methuen, Ma. the following Thursday afternoon at about 5:00 P.M. That was better time than I ever made by train or plane. The reason, of course, I was on the road 24/7 almost every day; I slept while the driver was awake. When the driver had to turn off my route or stop to eat or sleep, I bailed out and found me another ride. I also avoided those long waits at airport terminals and railroad stations between connections, which sometimes lasted all day. Of course, Route 66 no longer exists the way it was back then. The road has been changed to bypass all the major cities.

Here are some of the highlights of that trip as I remember it. I can no longer remember every single "lift" I got along the way; but I do remember the most significant ones. The first night out of California, I got two rides which took me through San Bernadino, Barstow, Needles and well into Arizona, by the next morning. In fact, the second ride was a man, traveling alone. He took me all the way to the Junction of Route 66 and the road that goes north to the Grand Canyon at Williams, slightly west of Flagstaff. He insisted that I accompany him, all expenses paid, on a tour of the south rim of the canyon. But I declined; I suspected that this guy was gay, but I never entertained any thoughts of being diverted from my chosen path. I picked up a ride into Flagstaff; then another into the desert near Holbrook, NM near a Navaho Indian Reservation. I was in the middle of nowhere; it was very hot and there wasn't very much traffic on the road that day. A light, blue Cadillac Convertible; top down, went by me in a cloud of dust, about 90 miles an hour. The automobile had traveled at least a half mile past me before I realized it had stopped to pick me up. I started running toward the Cadillac as it was backing up toward me. When it came along side, I noticed the rear license plate holder had the words "Coral Gables Florida" printed on it. I climbed into the front passenger seat and threw my duffle bag on the back seat. Then, I noticed an open bottle of Rye Whiskey setting in the space located between the front seats: there were no consoles between seats in those days. The driver asked me, "Where are you headed, Sailor?" I replied, "East Coast, New York City." He looked at me, took a swig of his whiskey and said, "I'm heading to Florida. You can go all the way with me or any part of it." We were now cruising about 90 miles an hour and he began to talk about himself. He told me that he was a Dealer from Vegas heading back to Florida for a visit. That he was divorced and that he had a boy which he had not seen in 10 years. He kept on talking and taking swigs from the bottle. He said that he thought maybe his son was in the Navy. As I listened to this guy's story, I realized that I had heard it before. I served with a sailor by the name of Jack Sayer when I was in the Aleutian Islands. Jack was, without a doubt, the best radio operator I had ever encountered. He was tall, handsome and he could play any musical instrument that he would pick up. Jack came from Coral Gables and he told me that his parents were divorced; and that his father was a dealer in Las Vegas. Jack Sayer was not an easy guy to forget. I'm thinking, as we're cruising through the desert, could this man who just picked me up, be Jack's father? As we were chatting, we drove through Gallup and Albuquerque, NM. I got an opportunity to speak, I casually said, "I knew only one person who claimed to be from Coral Gables, Fl." He asked me, "Yeh, who's that?." "Jack Sayer," I replied. The Cadillac almost left the road, he was so surprised by my response. He exclaimed, "Son of a bitch,! Jack Sayer is my son!" He asked me to describe him and he wanted to know how his son was getting on; remember he had not seen Jack in 10 years. I was able to fill him in pretty well because I had been stationed with Jack less than two years earlier. It was getting dark as we approached Santa Rosa, NM; so we stopped there for the night. Jack's father treated me to a Prime Rib steak dinner and a room in a near by motel. He came and wakened me early the next morning and bought me a huge, bacon & egg breakfast. Then, we hit the road east, again, at about 90 miles an hour. He kept trying to convince me to go to Florida with him. I insisted on sticking with Route 66, my designated course to New York City. That morning, he took me as far as, Amarillo, Tx; he headed south and east to New Orleans and on to Florida. I got back on the road there and almost immediately, got picked up by a couple who took me to Oklahoma City. When I got into the back seat of their car, the man driving says to me, "Man, you're doing better than we are!" "What do you mean," I replied. He proceeded to tell me that they saw me hitchhiking Sunday evening back in Pasadena, but they didn't pick me up because they assumed I wasn't going very far. They told me, then, they had seen me in a light blue, Caddy Convertible go by them at high speed in the desert the day before. They decided to give me a lift in Amarillo just to see where the heck I was going.

This couple was going from the Naval Air Station at North Island in San Diego to an Air Base in Norman, Ok. The man was a U.S. Navy flyer being transferred and his wife was traveling with him. When we got to Oklahoma City, they dropped me off in front of the state capitol building; in those days, Route 66 went right past the front door. They pointed out a place down the street where they recommended I stop for a bite to eat. This eatery was supposed to be the place where "Chicken-in-the-Basket" had been invented. I ate there and moved on. A Singer Sewing Machine salesman, in a panel truck, without much fanfare, took me from Oklahoma City to Tulsa. Somewhere, a few miles west of Joplin, Mo. I hooked up with a couple of interesting characters. Two fellows, sharing the driving, wearing civilian clothes: even though they were flyboys (USAF), driving a beat-up vintage car, picked me up. They told me right up front, that they were broke; having lost their cash at the tables in Las Vegas. They were bound for a very small town in the southeastern corner of Ohio; which I never heard of nor do I remember the name of. I did, however, know that their destination was located across the Ohio border from Wheeling, WVA. They did warn me that if the car broke down or if they ran out of gas, they would abandon it and start hitchhiking with me. We traveled east through St. Louis, Mo. and beyond. We left Route 66 at Springfield, Ill. and continued into Indiana which is probably Route 170 today. We motored through Terre Haute, IN and into Ohio at Dayton. We drove through Columbus, capitol of Ohio, Zaneville and St. Clairsville at the West Virginia border. These two guys were on the road 24 hours a day, swapping off the driving every 4 hours or so. They did not even stop to eat or sleep. They were traveling on a "shoestring." To ensure my passage, I purchased a couple of tanks of gas for them. In those days, you could fill the tank for about five bucks. They left me on the Ohio border, just west of Wheeling, early on a Wednesday evening. I had no trouble getting into Wheeling because there was a lot of traffic and activity there. "Ike" Eisenhower was campaigning in Wheeling that night for a shot in the next presidential election. I got a lift out of Wheeling over to the Pennsylvania Turnpike, at a couple of exits east of Pittsburgh. My ride was actually heading west, but he dropped me off at a Howard Johnson's Service Center which was located between East and Westbound lanes. I just walked through the Rest Area to the Eastbound side of the highway, where I found a "truckie" to take me east. I boarded a tanker truck that gave me a ride down the turnpike to Philadelphia and on to the truck terminals at the Brooklyn Battery.

From there, I had no problem catching a lift with a truck driver working for the same outfit as the one who drove me there; and then to the fuel terminals in Revere, Ma. In those days, there was no Route I95, I295 or I495; I hitchhiked up Route 1 to Route 114 to Middleton and Lawrence. I then caught a bus to Methuen. I was home! I got my kicks and also got to see a great deal of the country to boot.

CHAPTER 10

"Home on the Range"

I began living with my Aunt Jean and Uncle John at 5 Arnold Street; they lived on the 1st Floor, her sister, my Aunt Irene and her husband, my Uncle George lived on the 2nd Floor. I had a little "Dutch Flat" in the 3rd Floor attic space. I had the ability to come and go through the front door directly to the 3rd Floor; bypassing the first two floors. I could also use the back door to gain access to either one. I took my meals with Aunt Jean and she did my laundry for which, I paid her $20 a week. I beat my sea bag home from San Diego, no big surprise.

Upon discharge from the service, I received $300 mustering out pay from Uncle Sam; paid in $100 increments for 3 months and $300 from the Commonwealth of Massachusetts, paid in one lump sum, courtesy of Governor Christian Herter. The very first thing I purchased with that money was, a grey, double breasted, sharkskin suit. I bought it at Kap's Men Store on Essex Street in Lawrence. It cost me about $100.

I hung out for a few days resting up from my trip home. I soon learned that work was not easy to find in our area. I was very fortunate, at this point, because my Uncle John was able to get me employment as a laborer with Realty Construction Co. on Trapelo Road in Waltham, Ma. They were engaged in a huge project building veteran's housing out of a large plot of woodland off Trapelo Road. The project involved the construction of 250 homes from the ground up. My Uncle John was operating a bull dozer and a back hoe temporarily stored there on site for Paul Garabedian Construction Co. out of

Salem, NH. Paul Garabedian was sub-contracting his equipment plus an operator, my Uncle John, to Realty Construction. My uncle had worked for Paul for many years in various capacities. They had grown up and went to school together in the area. My Uncle George was already working there as a laborer. He and I ended up working directly for Realty and we commuted from Metheun to Waltham, free of charge, with Uncle John using Paul Garabedian's pickup truck. It was a real good deal because all three of us lived at the Arnold Street address. One street containing the model homes had already been built from which prospective buyers could choose. Then the buyer picked out his lot and we would come along, dig the cellar, pour the foundation and frame out the new house. We also cut new streets out of the woods to bring all the utilities; gas, water, telephone and electricity. There already were about 30 homes built and occupied when I started. That is what provided seed money to keep the project going. I worked there from late September until the first significant snowfall; after Thanksgiving, that year. I made an interesting observation while working on this project. Each time the bull dozer broke fresh ground the pheasant would come out of the woods and feast on the fresh supply of worms. When hunting season for pheasant opened, everyone on the project brought their shot guns to work. Guess what? Not a pheasant in sight! How did they know? An old timer on the project told me, "All those pheasant have to hear is the first gunshot and they are gone until Spring!"

With the money that I was earning from that job, I got caught up on my "room and board" and was able to buy some new clothes. I stayed pretty close to home through the Holiday Season that year. After the first of the new year, I began aggressively to search for permanent employment. One evening during this period, my Aunt Irene, who lived in the apartment just below me, yelled up the stairway, "Skip, you have a phone call!" I could not imagine who would be calling me, especially on my Aunt Irene's telephone. It was my old girl friend from Long Beach, Mary, checking up on me. She pleaded with me to come back to California. She even had a good job lined up for me at the shipyard there. I was tempted, but I refused. It occurred to me, "How did you locate me in the first place?" She said, "It was very simple. All I had to do was call the Naval Separation Center in San Diego and ask for the forwarding address you left." She went on to tell them that she was in possession of some of my personal belongings that she was attempting to return. With my address in hand, she proceeded on to a long distance operator to find any telephone numbers listed at that address. Turned out, there were two and both belonged to my aunts who lived at the same address that I did. She could not miss!. I learned a great deal from that experience about covering up my footsteps.

Soon after that, I got in touch with my old friend and neighbor from Hancock Street in Haverhill, Donald (Dumbo) Amaro. He was discharged from the U.S. Army about the same time as I was being separated from the U.S. Navy. Dumbo was the guy who used to walk to school and bum cigarettes from me every day.

We hooked up and went job hunting. He was still using his father's car, like in the old days. We looked everywhere, with no luck. I remember that we even tried getting into the Ford Plant in Somerville, Ma. It was then I realized how lucky I had been getting that job in Waltham with my Uncle John. Since I had gone in the Navy, most of the shoe shops in Haverhill had gone offshore or closed down.

The textile mills in Lawrence had all gone south. There was a huge force of skilled workers in the Merrimack Valley who were unemployed as a result. The Western Electric Company was the first large manufacturer to take advantage of the situation. In 1943, they began to transfer operations from their Kearney, NJ plant to Haverhill, where they occupied space in the Grad, Hayes and Winchell Buildings. In 1951, the Lawrence Shop opened up in the Monomac Mill Building in South Lawrence on South Union Street.

CHAPTER 11

"Call Me"

In February, 1953, I placed an application for employment with Western Electric in South Lawrence. A couple of weeks later, Muriel O'Brian, called me in to take a physical examination, a dexterity and an aptitude test. A few days later, on March 3, 1953, I was hired as a 33 Grade Relay Adjuster at $1.10 an hour. Who could have known that was the start of a 40 year career with Ma Bell, which saw me retire as a Senior Planning Engineer making about $85,000 a year, and I had never been to college a day in my life. Three other guys, who had been recently discharged from the military, were also hired as Relay Adjusters the very same day. They were Timmy Brennan, Denny Hines and Al Joncas. Timmy did not stay with Western Electric very long, but both Al and Denny ultimately became Shop Supervisors and retired at the same time I did. I moved along quickly to a 34 Grade Solderer and then to 34, 35 and 36 Grade Tester. On October 17, 1955, just 2 ½ years after I started out, I became a 37 Grade Test Set Technician. After becoming a Test Set Technician, I went from 37 to 40 Grade in less than 2 years. In June 1957, The union managed to get our whole universe re-classified, as "Skilled Tradesmen." As a result, I became a Class "A" Skilled Tradesman. I remained in that universe until I was promoted to an Engineering Associate on April 25, 1966.

In the summer of 1953, I decided to purchase an automobile. I was paying someone to drive me back and forth to work, but I still had to walk quite a ways to meet my driver. We met on the corner of Oakland Avenue and Broadway in Methuen each day. I bought a 1946 Mercury Convertible, which became a classic later on. This car was one of the very first manufactured after World War II. I bought it from Manzi Auto on Methuen Street in Lawrence. He wanted $500 for it; I told him if he put a new top (roof) and pads on it, he had a sale. Because I had not yet established my credit rating, I was forced to get my Uncle Duke to co-sign for me, which he did reluctantly. I put $100 down and agreed to make monthly installments. Al Joncas went with me to the Registry of Motor Vehicles in South Lawrence to obtain a Driver's License. In those days, the Inspectors would always take a new applicant to Brookfield Street in South Lawrence, a very steep hill and make you turn around on the hill, making only one pass. This was difficult because automobiles, in those days, all had stick shifts on the steering wheel and a clutch on the floor. No hill holders and no automatic transmissions. I did manage to pass the test on my first try, however.

On Sunday mornings, after I got my driver's license, I would go to South Lawrence and pick up Al Joncas on the corner near Sacred Heart Church and we would head to Hampton Beach for the day. I would park behind the Casino; change clothes and check them there in the bath house located right there in the Casino. Then, we would spend the entire day on the beach, enjoying the sun, water and the bikinis.

One Friday, when I was working the 2nd Shift at Western Electric, my Uncle Tony came to Methuen from Hadley around noon. He said, "Hey, Skip, let's go to the track!" I replied, "I can't, I have to go to work at 3:00 P.M." He responded, "Come with me just for the Daily Double. You take your car and I'll take mine. You can go to work whenever you want to," That's exactly what I expected to do. I could never refuse my Uncle Tony, he was always there for me.

But here is the rest of the story, as Paul Harvey used to say on the radio years ago. We got to Rockingham Race Track early enough to bet the Daily Double. I immediately purchased a $2.00 ticket on #5 and #3 because those were my father's favorite double numbers when I used to go the race tracks with him when I was 12 years old. He used to duck me under the turnstiles so he didn't have to pay for me. Then, I purchased a $6.00 Combine Ticket on the #5 horse, whose name was "Wish Egan," in the 1st Race, to back up my bet. My father had taught me to do that, as well. "Wish Egan" won the 1st Race handily and paid about $36.00 across the board. When the horses were leaving the paddock for the start of the 2nd Race, I noticed that the #3 horse (Brother March) was 60 to 1 on the tote board. When I met up with my Uncle Tony, back in the grandstand he told me the #7, Supercilious, was by far, the best horse in the 2nd Race. I returned to the betting windows and purchased a $6.00 Combine Ticket on Supercilious. When they announced the probable Daily Double payoffs; that is, the payoff of #5 coupled with every horse in the 2nd Race. The #5 horse coupled with #3 horse would pay $720.40. I ran to the window and bought a $2.00 win ticket on the #3 horse, Brother March in the 2nd Race, again, to back up my bet. When the horses were coming down the stretch, Supercilious (#7) was leading all the way to the wire. At the wire, however, another horse had slipped in on the rail, creating a photo finish. I was yelling and screaming for the #7 horse, Supercilious to win because I was holding a $6.00 Combine Ticket ($2.00 across the board) on him. My Uncle Tony shouted at me, "That was your #3 horse on the rail, you Dummy!" Holy mackerel, now I am praying for the #3 horse to win the race and it did! Wow, I played only two races and I made a killing. I had already collected $36.00 for cashing the combo ticket in the 1st Race and then, I collected $720.40 for the $2.00 double ticket (#5 & #3); $122.80 for the $2.00 win ticket on #3 in the 2nd Race and finally; $12.40 for place and show on the combo ticket on the #7 in the 2nd Race. At this point, I was $891.60 ahead of game. Needless to say, I did not go to work that afternoon. It took me so long to cash all my winning tickets, I missed a chance to bet on the 3rd Race. I was back in action for the 4th Race; I just could not lose that day. I cashed a few more winning tickets before going home and plunking twelve $100 dollar bills down on my Aunt Jean's kitchen table.

My uncle and I went out celebrating that night, on me, of course. I did not go back to the track the next day, Saturday; I went to work instead. My uncle did go back and lost more money. Guess what, I would have made money the next day, as well, because the #5 and #3 horses won the Daily Double again; the payoff was a couple hundred dollars. I surely would have bought at least one $2.00 ticket on that combination again.

The following Monday morning, bright and early, I went right down to Manzi's and paid off the balance on my convertible, about $350 and brought the receipt to my Uncle Duke, letting him off the hook as the co-signer. That convertible was really a great car for getting the girls. They would scream and call after me as I drove down the street. One evening, at Hampton Beach, there were guys and gals hanging all over the car as I drove along the boulevard. A cop stopped me right in front of the bandstand for operating an overloaded vehicle. By the time he pulled me over, most of my passengers had disappeared into the crowd. The policeman gave me a warning and suggested that I would not drive an overloaded vehicle in Methuen. He was right, of course.

When I worked overtime on the 2nd Shift at Western Electric, I would not leave the plant until approximately 1.00 A.M. I would drive up to Salem, N.H. to the Monarch Diner on Broadway and Kelley's Crossing for breakfast. I always ordered two dropped (poached) eggs on toast with home fries and coffee. The short-order cook there always made perfect dropped eggs; stiff whites and runny yolks. One night, I asked him how he accomplished that so consistently every time. He told me, "It's really very simple; just bring the water to a rolling boil in a shallow pan; add a couple drops of white vinegar and turn the heat off. Drop two eggs into the water, basting them with a table spoon until the whites get stiff.

Remove and drain the eggs with a perforated spatula, one egg at a time, and place each egg on a piece of golden brown toast." I have followed this procedure since then and it has always produced perfect results. The vinegar makes the whites stiffen early leaving runny yolks. People have been wondering, all these years, how I manage to produce perfect poached eggs. There's the answer!

At this particular time in my life, I was seeing two lady friends; one, was a girl named Terry from Derry, N.H. and the other was Penny from Methuen. Over the years, no matter when I came to town, I would bump into Penny and we'd end up going out somewhere together. The day I purchased the new suit at Kaps Men's Store, which I mentioned earlier, I ran into her as I was leaving the store. Seems like everywhere I went, there she was also. I was working nights on the 2nd Shift, testing Crystal Filters on the fifth floor in the AC Room in the South Lawrence Plant and I was studying AC-DC Theory in order to pass the tests necessary to qualify for Testing Positions up to 37 Grade.

After passing all those tests, I went on into the Radio Theory Tests which would qualify me for positions up to 40 Grade Test Set Technician. I wanted to be ready in case any future up-grades became available to me and they eventually did. My strategy was to accept any up-grade, regardless of shift or location because that would allow me to by-pass a lot of people at that level who had more seniority than I did. Then, I would be placed at the top of the eligibility list for subsequent up-grades. This is exactly what happened to me at some point. My strategy worked! When I was working the 2nd Shift as a 35 Grade Tester; a 36 Grade opening occurred on the 3rd Shift for which I was qualified. There were many qualified people with more seniority than I had, but no one wanted to go on the 3rd Shift, I accepted that job and a few days before I was report for that 3rd Shift assignment; another opening appeared for a 37 Grade Test Set Technician on days (1st Shift)! I was the only qualified candidate on the list because I left the rest of the pack back at the 35 Grade level. I moved, therefore, from a night shift tester to a day shift technician, opening up a new universe of opportunities for myself. I always advise, as a rule of thumb, that young people always accept promotions or upward movement, even if it means a change of venue; such as, a new department at the same location or even at another location.

CHAPTER 12

"At Last"

On July 17, 1954, after a rather brief courtship, I married my first wife, Pauline Boisvert (Penny). She had been married before and was divorced. Penny had lost her first child, a baby boy named, "Bobby". She was living in a third floor apartment on Springfield Street in South Lawrence. I was still living on Arnold Street in Methuen on the third floor of my Aunt Jean's house. We were married in Saint Joseph's Catholic Church in Salem, N.H. We had a small, but nice wedding reception at Penny's Auntie Helen's house on Tower Hill in Lawrence.

It was held outdoors in a large backyard there. We moved into a small, one bedroom apartment on South Broadway just below Kelly's Crossing. The apartment was situated over a store front for Larry's Woodworking Company; the shop was located in a building behind the store. We went on our honeymoon to Lake Winnapasaukee at the Wise Owl Motor Court along the lake east of the Weirs. We had our first argument there! Penny was working days at a shoe shop in Lawrence on Canal Street and I was working nights at Western Electric. I remember "Hurricane Carol" came through in late September that year (1954); I had to go into Lawrence to bring Penny home from work in that storm. I did not go to work that night. That storm did a great deal of damage throughout the Merrimack Valley.

Early in my employment at Western Electric, the hourly workers voted to become a "union shop." I became an active member of the Communication Workers of America (CWA). We went on strike one year for better wages, vacations and health benefits. I went to work for Rene Damphouse Roofing and Sidewall Company in South Lawrence on Mount Vernon Street to "keep bread on the table." I worked for Rene Damphouse doing tar and gravel roofing. I had previous experience doing this kind of work. When I was a kid living on Hancock Street in Haverhill, my landlord, a Jewish guy, named Barney Levenson, owned his own roofing business; he operated out of the garages located behind the tenement we rented from him. I used to help him out, especially on small jobs repairing leaks in inclement weather. I learned how to use the "brake and shears," to bend and cut the galvanized metal gravel skirts that run around the edge of a flat roof to prevent the small stones (gravel) from falling off the roof. I am also a proficient "kettle tender."

This is the person who cuts open the containers of asphalt (tar) with an axe, chops it into small enough pieces to fit in the tank or kettle to be melted into molten tar. Then the "hot," as it is called, is hoisted to the roof with a motorized or manually operated chain fall to be employed to waterproof the roof by sealing the layers of felt paper which are placed over the scraped down, bare roof. The molten tar is then poured over the tarpapered roof to set the gravel in place. I also had to learn how to solder the seams in the galvanized gravel skirt. I came to the job with a lot of experience and it is hard work, especially on hot summer days. The thing I disliked most about that job was the manner in which we were paid. Every Friday evening, after the regular work day, the crew would meet at Manny Lavoie's Tavern on South Broadway and wait until Rene Damphouse got damn good and ready to bring our pay checks. Most of the guys were so thirsty they would start drinking and running a tab until their checks arrived. Of course, Manny was prepared to cash these checks at the bar; withholding a good deal of their money which was spent even before the checks got there. I always thought Manny and Rene had a kickback program going on between them. It was very hard to just hang around without having at least two draft beers. By the way, the strike was very effective; we made quite a few gains in the ensuing contract.

On January 2, 1956 our first child, a girl; which we named Angela Jeanne Biron was born. For those who were counting, she was born 18 months after we were married. Angela was almost a New Years day baby. Penny's water broke on January 1st, New Years day about four in the afternoon, while I was watching one of the bowl, football games on TV. I remember running around behind her with a mop. We had no telephone, so I ran up the street to Bob Davis's house to call the doctor's emergency answering service. Dr. Mallen called right back and said, "Get her to the Bon Secours Hospital right now. I'll meet you there." Penny went into labor right away, but the baby was stubborn, refusing to come into the world before mid-night. There would be no New Years baby. They told me to go home, get some sleep and wait it out. I no sooner got home and Bob Davis was pounding on my door. He told me that I was the father of a new, baby girl. I turned right around and went back to the hospital just in time to see the nurse taking our baby from the delivery room into the nursery. I remember thinking, what a bloody mess she was; they had not yet cleaned her up. When I went into the room where Penny was recovering, she asked me, "Did you see him?" I said, "Yes, I saw her. It's a girl!" She said, "I know, but did you see him?" She was sure that Angela was going to be a boy. Some days later, when I saw that my Angela had beautiful, brown, almond eyes, I began to sing, "Beautiful, beautiful brown eyes; I'll never love blue eyes again!" Angela was born hungry. We had her eating Gerber's Baby Food so soon that most of our friends thought we were crazy. Another thing about this child: when she was very fussy and could not or would not sleep, I would get right into the crib with her; hug and sing to her and off she would go into dreamland. She no doubt became a "Daddy's girl." The place we were living was too small. The crib was actually in the living room. So we moved back to Massachusetts; into a two bedroom apartment with an archway type living room/parlor combination and eat-in kitchen. It was located on Mann Street in the Prospect Hill section of Lawrence. We occupied the first floor and the land lord lived on the second floor. There was a nice, big yard on one side of the building. It was situated on a steep hill and parking was a huge problem, especially in the winter, when the off-street parking ban was enforced. We were comfortable there for a couple of years. Penny stopped working and became a stay-at-home Mom. I was doing well at Western Electric. By this time, I was a 40 Grade Test Set Technician working in the Bell Laboratories wing of the new building being erected in North Andover on Osgood Street. I was "moonlighting" at the time, as well, fixing televisions, car radios and small appliances. I was forced to trade in the 1946 Mercury Convertible for a family style car. The old "Merc" was too cold in the winter and girls were still calling after me as I drove by; which did not please Penny very much. So I bought a brand new 1957 Studebaker Scotsman from Eddie Dupont on South Broadway in Lawrence. The "Scotsman" was an automobile produced by the Studebaker-Packard Corp. of South Bend, Indiana and as the name implies, was based on the reputation of Scottish frugality. The car was built for function with minimal luxury. Despite it's austerity, the Scotsman delivered exceptional value and economy; the small, six cylinder engine delivered 30 miles per gallon (MPG) of gas with over-drive transmission. This was unheard of mileage for a car of it's size in 1957. Nothing fancy, just reliable, low cost transportation.

Just when things seemed to be going well, the union (CWA) called another strike. The company stopped negotiating the new contract and they did not think that we would vote to strike again. But we did! This time, I went to work for Pat-Laur Italian Bakery in South Lawrence delivering Italian bread and pastry to many variety stores and homes in the Lawrence area. I also delivered bread and pastry on a daily basis to the Track Kitchen at Rockingham Race Track in Salem, N.H. This was my largest account. The Track Kitchen was where all the people working at the track, were served; the owners, jockeys, trainers, stable hands, hot walkers and grooms. This strike lasted longer than the first; but it was equally as effective. When it ended, I went back to work, as usual, to my Western Electric/Bell Laboratories position. Now, I was called and paid as a a Class A Skilled Tradesman, instead of a 40 Grade Test Set Technician. The new union contract included some major changes to the pay structure which basically, that meant, all 40 and 41 Grade Technicians became Class A Skilled Tradesmen; all 38 and 39 Grade Technicians became Class B Skilled Tradesmen; all 37 Grade technicians became Class C Skilled Tradesmen. The change included a substantial raise, created a new category and a new "ceiling" for the entire universe. The new contract addressed other issues dealing with paid vacations and health insurance, as well.

While living on Mann Street, even though Angela was only 3 years old, I became active with all the older kids in the neighborhood. I mounted a basket and net on the corner; so I could play basketball (hoops) with all the older boys and girls in the neighborhood. We played "one-on-one," or "horse;" sometimes we would play to see who was the best free throw (foul line) shooter. We played "tag rush" (touch) football, as well.

During baseball season, using the field adjacent to the house I was renting, I pitched batting practice to a couple of the older boys. I worked on their batting skills so they might become "switch hitters;" that is, boys who were able to hit both left and right handed. There was a teen aged boy; Bobby Lauterbach and his sister, Karen; who lived next door that played in the Lawrence High School Band. Bobby played the drums and Karen was a majorette. One day when I was obviously at home, but had failed to come out after supper; Bobby came knocking at our back door. My wife, Penny answered the door and he asked her, "Oh, hello Mrs. Biron, can Mr. Biron come out to play with us?"

In 1960, my Uncle George, my Aunt Irene's husband died and my aunt moved out of her second floor tenement on Arnold Street and went to live with her daughter, my cousin Jan and her husband, Harry Zakarian on Olive Street in the Methuen east end. My Aunt Jean and Uncle John, who were living on the first floor, fixed up the second floor tenement and moved upstairs. Then, I moved into the vacated first floor tenement with Penny and Angela after appropriate renovations were completed. I ended up living on the first floor in the same building on Arnold Street that I had occupied the third floor flat when I came home from the Navy about five years earlier.

CHAPTER 13

"Stranger in Paradise"

Soon things in my life became very tenuous. My aunt and my wife did not see "eye to eye" on many issues. We began to argue about everything. At one point, we separated. Because I could not bear to be separated from my family, I made several concessions to get them back at my side. We mutually decided that maybe we could make a go of it, if we bought our own place and moved out of my Aunt Jean's house. I went out and bought an old Cape Cod house with two, good sized bedrooms upstairs. It was located at 3 Tenney Street at the end of Kirk Street in Methuen. The seller wanted $8000, which was a lot of money in those days. My counter offer was $6900, which they accepted. I used $1600 worth of AT&T Stock, which I had acquired during my first few years at Western Electric, as the down payment. The monthly payment was; $39.00 which covered the principal, interest and taxes; that the bank withheld in escrow without paying interest. That was well within the general rule; that, your monthly mortgage payment will not exceed one week's pay or 25% of your monthly salary. I believe that is still a valid guideline in today's world. The first major issue which had to be addressed, was to replace the old, coal and wood burning furnace in the cellar with a new furnace. Because there was no bulkhead, removing the old furnace required use of an acetylene torch to cut it up in small enough pieces to pass through a small cellar window. A new natural gas furnace with a built-in humidifier was assembled in the same manner; by passing the parts through the same window and assembling it on the cellar floor. Next, waterproofing the fieldstone foundation was required to eliminate the water in the cellar.

Then I paneled and wall papered throughout the house and installed vinyl tile on most of the floors. I developed many new building skills and saved a ton of money by doing all the work myself. In the cellar, I built myself a large work bench with terraced shelves and draws; it was essentially a complete work station. I designed it so that it could be disassembled and moved to another house by passing the parts through the cellar window just like we did with the furnace. We were not planning to stay there forever. I was still doing TV and radio repair work and the new bench provided a much better place to work than the kitchen table, which is where I had been working all along. I built all my own test equipment; a signal generator, a signal tracer, an oscilloscope, a vacuum tube voltmeter (VTVM) and a capacitor checker. I purchased and built all these instruments by myself. The instruments were all purchased from Heathkit, which was a company that supplied parts and assembly instructions for the Do-it-Yourselfer, in kit form. I had designed my new work bench with shelves to house these instruments surrounding a large, centralized work area making it easy to trouble shoot and repair broken TVs and such. With the help of my friend and lead engineer at Western, Ray DeMatteo, we tore down the old wooden front stoop and stairs and replaced it with a larger, concrete stoop and brick stairs. The last major project was to side-wall the exterior of house.

We became "envelope contributing" members of Saint Monica's Church in Methuen. It was just about the time that church was engaged in a new project to build a parochial school. We pledged the prescribed amount for each family in the parish to ensure a seat for Angela in the first Grade One class. The school was a two story building with the first level housing classrooms; the nuns occupied the second floor. Angela started school there in 1963 in a class of 50 students. Actually, they began with two classes of 50 and continued each subsequent year trying to maintain that quota. Soon we were pledging funds to build a new convent for the nuns; they had run out of first floor classroom space. Angela spent her first eight years of education there and became part of the first class to graduate from

Saint Monica's School. It is very interesting to note that daughters of men that I worked with at Western Electric were also part of Angela's class and became her friends. There was Paula Geary who was the daughter of George Geary, a supervisor in the Drafting Department and a friend of mine. There was Gene Dimariano's daughter, Diane, another one of Angela's classmates and friends. Gene and I were Test Set Technicians together in our early days at Western Electric. Many years later, Gene became my Department Chief when I was working as an Engineering Associate in a Transmission Systems Consulting group.

In 1964, I traded my Studebaker Scotsman in for a new Studebaker Wagonaire. This car was manufactured in Hamilton, Ontario, Canada, because the South Bend, Indiana, Studebaker Plant had shut down. This model of station wagon featured a retractable roof section that allowed the vehicle to carry items that would otherwise be too tall for a conventional station wagon of that era; such as, a standard refrigerator in the upright position. The major problem with this new design was that the roof leaked around the sliding panel. As far as I know, the problem was addressed by the factory, but never successfully repaired. I did a great deal of work for myself and others with this automobile because with the rear seat folded down and the sliding roof positioned forward, it was very similar to a pickup truck. The Wagonaire seated 6 passengers and became a conventional station wagon when the rear seat was placed upright and the roof was moved back to it's normal position.

While living on Tenney Street, our yard became a hangout for all the neighborhood children. On hot summer days and evenings, I would hook up the garden hose and spray them to cool them down. I filled the wagon with kids and traveled down to the Neal Playstead to play baseball; I would make two trips, if necessary. On one occasion, I took Angela and some of the neighborhood kids up to the Castle in the Clouds in Moultonboro, N.H. for a day trip. Another excursion I used to make with the kids was to go up to Belknap Mountain; I think it's called Gunstock now, take the chair lift to the top and fill up buckets with lots of nice big, high bush blueberries. We ate a lot of berries on the mountain, but still managed to bring enough home to make a pie or two and some muffins. There were kids, from 6 to 16, hanging out on my front steps all the time.

We talked about all the things that young people had on their minds. I was always honest and out in the open with them and I never avoided any of their questions. I am sure we discussed things that they dared not talk to their parents about. One boy, Billy Howard, who lived on the third floor of the triple decker next door with 3 brothers and 2 sisters, ended up marrying our niece, Donna from East Hartford, CT. This was a result of meeting while hanging out on my front steps. Billy was also our paper boy; he delivered the Lawrence Eagle Tribune to our house on a daily basis. It should be obvious by now that no matter where I lived or how old my own children were, the neighborhood children and young adults hung out on my front doorstep. I just seemed to attract these children or maybe they attracted me, but somehow we always managed to get together. It was the very same with my Dad before me and my brother, Buddy, after me. Maybe it is in our genes.

It was on these same front steps where Angela used to tell all the passers by that, "My Daddy can fix anything. Just leave your broken things here. If he don't fix them, you pay nothing!" I managed to always satisfy my customers; that is and always has been my goal. I had to be the best at everything I did. I became very proficient in repairing all kinds of things; televisions, radios, car radios, stereos, record players, toasters, washers and dryers.

I had also developed a very good business installing television antennas on rooftops, chimneys and sides of buildings all over the Merrimack Valley. Cable Television was not yet available in the area making an outdoor antenna necessary for anyone who wanted to receive good reception. I usually used the type of arrangement where the mast of the array would be strapped to the chimney up on the roof. Before Cable TV became affordable, I installed the "directional antenna" which was motor driven and operated by a customer in the home; to be rotated in the direction of the transmitting station for optimum reception. For example, the antenna could be oriented toward Boston to receive the four or five channels which emanated from there. To Channel 9 from Manchester, N.H. or Channel 11 from UNH in Durham, N.H.; the antenna required rotation of about 180 degrees for best reception. To receive Channel 6 from Portland, Me.; rotation in the opposite direction somewhat less than 180 degrees was required. Depending on the location of the home relative to the source of the transmitting signal, remote areas of the country not served by a Cable TV carrier, are still employing this type of antenna system.

I was able to earn a good deal of money "under the table" by "moonlighting" from my Western Electric position because I was able to purchase most of my parts and materials in quantity and at wholesale prices at a local Electrical Outlet store and also because I had built up a good reputation for being competent and reasonably priced. I never advertised; relying entirely on "word of mouth" recommendations from satisfied customers. Some of my customers absolutely refused to go any place else for service, regardless of how long they had to wait. If I was out of town on business or just unavailable for any reason, they would leave the broken TV on my back porch with a note telling me who had left it and a phone number to call when it was ready to pick up.

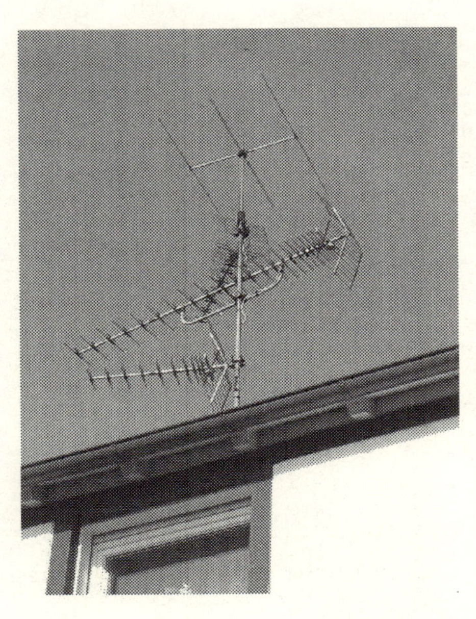

CHAPTER 14

"My Buddy"

One evening in 1961 or 1962, I can't remember which, but it was while living on Tenney Street, the phone rang and Penny ran to answer it. She shouted to me from the kitchen wall phone. "Hon, it's your brother, Buddy!" she cried out to me. I immediately thought, I have not seen or heard from my brother in over 12 years. Where is he? What does he want? I jumped up and ran to the telephone and sure enough, it was my long lost brother! I even recognized his voice. "Where are you?" I asked. He told me that he was in North Andover.....that he was traveling with a basketball team from Berkshire Christian College in Lenox, Ma. where he was studying to be a minister......that he was staying at the home of a family whose son played basketball for Gordon University, another Christian School in Massachusetts that was to be their next opponent of their current road trip. I asked to speak with someone in charge to obtain their address and to obtain permission to take my brother home with me on an "overnight pass." It turned out that he was staying with a family that lived on Bay State Road in North Andover which is located just up Osgood Street from Western Electric, where I was working at the time. They didn't even need to give me directions; just the house number. I picked up my brother and took him home with me to Tenney Street; promising to get him back the next morning before 9:30 A.M.

Penny was amazed by how much alike we were; we looked alike, acted alike, spoke and gestured alike. He walked my old, wooden rocking chair right across the living room floor, just as I did. He filled me in on what happened to himself and our sister, Norma; since that morning when I left his bedside, 12 years earlier, to go into the U.S. Navy. He explained how they got from Haverhill, Ma. to Jacksonville, Fl. How they moved from High Street in Haverhill to Oakland Avenue in Methuen to the third floor in Uncle Dukey's triple decker there. How he went to the Steven Grammar School and then to the Searles Junior High and then, he and Dad moved to Ryan's Manor before sneaking off to Jacksonville, Fl. under the cover of darkness. He told me that he and Norma both graduated from high school in Florida; Buddy from Andrew Jackson and Norma from Paxton. My sister worked at the Prudential Insurance Co. which was headquartered there at the time. The Prudential Tower in Boston had not yet been built. When the Boston site opened, many of the Jacksonville people transferred; my sister remained in Jacksonville. She married Billy Carter, who became a Baptist preacher, and had one son, Michael at the time Buddy delivered his up-date. After Buddy and I re-connected; Penny, Angela and I frequently visited him in Lenox, Ma. We met his future wife, Gracia Cook, who was also going to school at Berkshire Christian; ultimately attended their wedding in Winslow, Me. on June 29, 1963. Buddy and Gracia were just starting their Junior year at college; they visited us often on Tenney Street, after they were married. We also attended his graduation ceremonies from Berkshire Christian College in 1965. On April 25, 1966, I was promoted from a Class "A" Skilled Tradesman to an Engineering Associate. This was a huge milestone because a minimum of two years of college had always been a prerequisite for entry into the engineering universe. I had none. I had been assigned to Bell Telephone Laboratories equipment pool for five or six years with my head pressed up "against the ceiling" and nowhere to go. The two year requirement was waived in favor of experience in a few cases because the demand for qualified Engineering Associates exceeded the supply. It certainly opened a great opportunity for me. Being an opportunist from day one at Western Electric, I really took advantage of the situation and moved right on up in the new engineering universe. Walt Steibitz, the guy who "took a chance" with me, was my new Department Chief and soon became my mentor and friend. He had plans for me and I did not disappoint him. More about our friendship and working relationship will follow in the chapters ahead.

In the summer of 1967, my sister, Norma and her family, visited us on Tenney Street. In addition to her son, Michael; she now had a daughter, Amanda; we called her "Mandy." I showed her around the area where she had been born and raised; including a visit to our mother's grave site at the Linwood Cemetery in Haverhill. Of course, she had never known her mother. I also took her to visit our Aunt Jean and Uncle John with whom she had been living when our father whisked her off to Florida.

In 1969, my grandmother (Memiere) Biron passed away in a nursing home on Tower Hill in Lawrence, Ma. She was 85 years old. My cousin, Maureen and I, had gone there to visit shortly before she died. During that visit, Memiere told us the story of her life. How my grandfather (Pepiere), George Biron, had gone to Sherbrooke, Canada and took her from a convent there and married her. She said she was just fifteen years old at the time. She laughingly confessed that if she had known what was going to happen to her, she probably would not have married my grandfather at all. She had a lot of children; only 11 of them survived. All of her children were born at home. Many died in childbirth or from miscarriages. She told us that she had two sets of twins born in the same calendar year and none of them survived. Because none of her children were born in a hospital, their birth records got all messed up. It wasn't until many years later that the children learned that some of them bore the surname, Biron (with the "i") and some, Byron (with the "y"); depending on how the midwife or doctor chose to spell their last name when submitting the information for the birth certificate at city hall.

My Uncle Tom and Uncle Tony did not know their surname was Byron, with the "y", until World War II began; when they needed a birth certificate to join the U.S. Army. My father's name, as well as my own, has always been, Biron, with the "i" .

CHAPTER 15

"Those Were the Days"

My grandmother Biron's death had a very significant effect on the remainder of the family. Her husband, my grandfather, died of cancer in 1942, when I was 12 years old; while living on the second floor at Brown Street in Methuen. He died at home after having been ill for a very long time. There was no cure for cancer and no money for hospital care. His wake and funeral were also conducted from home. I can remember the entire scenario, even now. I also remember that his death was responsible for splitting the Biron family into two camps. The dispute centered around which of his possessions went to whom. He had no money; all he had were a few "things" to divvy up among his kids. The family remained separated for about 27 years until my Memiere died. Her death had the opposite effect on the family. It brought the Biron family back together for ever. My brother, Buddy and I, played a major role in the "reunion" occurring. What actually happened; after my grandmother's funeral at Saint Monica's Church in Methuen, the family gathered at the VFW Hall, just up the street on Broadway. Every member of the Biron "clan" was there! All my uncles and aunts and their spouses; their children and their spouses and their grandchildren and their spouses. Over a hundred people were there; uncles, aunts and cousins that I had not seen in years and some that I had never seen. Everyone was actually enjoying being together as one, big family. Just before we were about to break up and go our own way, Buddy came up to me and said, "Isn't this wonderful, everyone coming together like this as a family?" Then, he said something that inspired me to respond, "If we could only get together like this more often." I thought; this crowd would probably not listen to Buddy or me. So we approached our Uncle Tony and asked him what he thought about starting a family reunion. He loved the idea! He grabbed the microphone and got everyone's attention and made a proposal. He even offered to host the first reunion at his farm in Hadley, Ma. and so, my grandmother Biron's death not only reunited the family, but helped to establish the Biron Family Reunion for the next four years. The first, in 1970, was at Uncle Tony's farm in Hadley, Ma; the second, in 1971, at Uncle Tom's in South Boston, Va.; the third, at Uncle Duke's summer home at Little Squam Lake, N.H. and the fourth, in Jacksonville, Fl. at my father's place.

CHAPTER 16

"Breaking Up is Hard to Do"

In 1970, my daughter, Angela, was attending Saint Mary's High School in Lawrence; studying Modern Jazz, Ballet and Tap Dancing with the Alice Franz Dance Studio in Lawrence and my wife, Penny and I were drifting farther and farther apart. I was on the road, traveling a great deal because of my job at Western Electric, staying away from home. It became obvious to me that she had found someone else. Her new "friend" was on the road a lot, as well. I learned about this guy quite by accident one day, when I found a letter addressed to Penny in our mail box from an unknown sender. I thought, at the time, that it was very careless of them to communicate by mail using our home address. Then, I thought, perhaps, they wanted to get caught. In any event, I developed a plan where I would catch them together, expose and confront them; which I finally did. It came down like this: I asked around about the guy, whose name I learned from the letter which I intercepted. I also found out where my wife was going every Tuesday night. In those days; the stores in Lawrence stayed open until 10:00 P.M. on Tuesday night. Her night out was Tuesday and mine was Friday when I was not out on the road. She would go out right after supper supposedly shopping; she began coming home later and later as time went by; often under the influence of alcohol. Soon, she was not getting home until two or three in the morning. Whoever was driving her home, was not leaving her off in front of our house; because in the summer when all the windows were open, I could hear the sound of her footsteps in high-heeled shoes coming down Tenney Street from the corner of Center Street. One

Tuesday night, after Angela was in bed sleeping, I locked up the house and went looking for them. They never thought I would leave her alone; that was part of their cover. They thought also, that I didn't know where their meeting place was located. A mutual friend of ours tipped me off one day, by accident. So I found them sitting at the bar in a very obscure club on Union Street near the Lawrence General Hospital.

When I confronted them, they seemed somewhat relieved. We agreed to separate. I stayed in the house on Tenney Street and continued paying down the mortgage; we were still joint owners. She re-located to an apartment on Broadway in Lawrence. I maintained a bedroom for Angela in my house even though we agreed that Angela would live with her mother. I paid my daughter's "room and board" weekly; paid for her dancing lessons and costumes, shoes etc., and her Parochial School tuition at Saint Mary's, her school uniforms and books. I continued to carry her Health Insurance through my employer. I even purchased a new refrigerator for Penny's new apartment so that I didn't have to move the old one from Tenney Street. We lived apart like that for quite a while, even after I met my second wife, Georgette.

CHAPTER 17

"The Second Time Around"

It was around 1970-1971, that I met my second wife, Georgette. The circumstances surrounding our first meeting were very unusual. The following information, I learned many years after we got together. At least five years before I met her, she worked on the second shift at Western Electric in North Andover; living in Hampton, N.H. with her first husband and their two sons. I was working there as well, but we never met. She had a friend, Rita Archie, who lived in Hampton and who also worked the second shift at Western Electric. They commuted back and forth to work with a third party. Late in 1963, Georgette's husband took his own life by carbon monoxide poisoning; locking himself in his own car with the tailpipe blocked and the motor running. He left her pregnant with a third child and two teenaged boys. Soon after, Rita Archie's husband was killed by a truck which backed up over him, while working for the Town of Hampton. The two friends were widowed at about the same time.

Georgette quit working to have her third son, Dana, who was born on her birthday, February 18, 1964. Rita continued to work and began to keep company with a friend of mine, who also was working at WECo. Rita was constantly asking my buddy if he knew anyone who may be interested in meeting her girl friend, Georgette. Finally our meeting was arranged; it developed into a relationship which lasted until she died, 45 years later. When we met; her son, Dana was 4 years old. They were living on Calumet Road in the Pleasant Valley section of Methuen in a little Cape Cod house, which she was renting. She was collecting a widows pension from her husband's Social Security and some support for herself and Dana from the Veteran's Administration (VA). The two older boys married and left her alone with Dana.

As our relationship developed, I began helping her more and more; taking most of my meals at her house when I was in town. I was still supporting my daughter, who was living with her mother. I paid my first wife for Angela's room and board every week. I also paid for Angela's parochial school tuition, uniforms and books; all of her dancing school expenses and all of her medical and dental expenses; including orthodontics (braces) to straighten her teeth. I maintained the house on Tenney Street as my permanent address with all the expenses associated with that situation; including, taxes, insurance, gas, lights, telephone, etc. My friends began to wonder how on earth was I managing all that responsibility. speak nothing about the expense involved. I sometimes wondered about it myself; I had learned very early in my life, you do what you have to do. Someone once said; "You can't plan your life, your life plans you. If you stay loose and roll with the punches, you will not only survive, but you will succeed."

Following are several significant events which occurred during this period of my life: I remember buying Dana his first two-wheeled bicycle without training wheels; and, running up and down Calumet Road teaching him how to ride it. It didn't take him very long and he was on his own. I remember Angela and her girl friend, Rita Nesbit, riding their bicycles from Broadway in Lawrence all the way to Calumet Road in Methuen to visit Georgette and Dana. Georgette would prepare lunch and provide cold drinks for them. The two girls would visit and play with Dana before returning home. I remember one snowy Christmas Eve when I drove Jet; that's what I called Georgette by this time, and Dana, to her brother Chippy's home located at Corbet's Pond in Windhan, N.H. for a family get together. We stayed late and the snow got very deep. I had to carry both Dana and Jet to the car while attempting to walk through waist deep snow. Jet had a few drinks too many which made the task even more difficult. When we arrived back home, Jet fell into the Christmas tree making a huge mess. I put them both to bed and restored the tree the best I could.

All four of us; Jet, Dana, Angela and I, going on picnics and swimming at Forrest Lake in Methuen and to Salisbury and Hampton Beaches. I remember the four of us going sledding in the winter on a hill near the Presentation of Mary Academy in Methuen. Looking back, we did a lot of fun things as a family. Angela became the daughter Georgette always wanted and Dana, became the son I always wanted. I became the father he never had. Dana started public school in the first grade at the Sergeant School in Methuen. He started school very young without ever attending preschool or kindergarten, which probably is why he became a "late bloomer."

At this time, I was confronted with the possibility that Jet was becoming an alcoholic. This problem almost broke us up early in our relationship. I suggested that she not drink alone; she was free to drink only when we were together. She agreed and it worked out so well, neither of us ever got drunk again.

CHAPTER 18

"My Blue Heaven"

Then Jet was asked to move from the place she was renting on Calumet Road. Apparently, the landlord wanted to finish off the expansion attic and rent the cottage out to someone in their own family. We found a two bedroom apartment on Grace Terrace in the Prospect Hill section of Lawrence. I bought a brand new queen sized bedroom set with a mirrored, triple dresser and a twin/bunk bed set for Dana's room. I have purchased several mattresses and box springs for the queen sized bed, but I still have that set and I still sleep on that bed; it is at least 40 years old and still in excellent condition. We transferred Dana to the Storrow School in Lawrence for Grades Two and Three.

Our relationship did not always enjoy smooth sailing; but, we always managed to negotiate the stormy seas together. Dana became the son I always wanted and Angela became the daughter that Jet always wanted. I became the father that Dana needed. We all needed one another at the time. This was another phase of my "care taking" duties.

Soon, my career took off. I got promotions and frequent raises. I won awards and received international recognition. Life was good!

Georgette became my inspiration! We stayed at Grace Terrace for 3 or 4 years, 1971-1975. Dana moved on to the Bruce School where he attended Grades Four through Six. During those years, Dana became an altar boy at St. Laurence O'Toole's Catholic Church. This was his own idea; he came to me one day and asked what I thought about it. We went down to see Father Halphen to find out what was involved. The next thing I know, he's carrying his cassock and surplice each weekday morning to serve the early Mass before school. At about the same time, he also decided to get involved in the public school music program. I took him down to the Oliver School to meet Mr. Palvino, who was the Lawrence Public School music director, to choose a musical instrument. The deal was: the student chooses the instrument he would like to play; he gets free music lessons during the entire school year. At the end of the year, the student gets an opportunity to purchase the instrument at a reduced price or return it at no cost. Mr. Palvino told me to let him walk along the table where the various musical instruments were on display to see what instrument he was attracted to. He picked up an old, B-Flat, silver trumpet and decided that was what he wanted to learn how to play. At the end of that school year, he elected to keep the trumpet and to continue playing. Naturally, I bought it for him. He continued studying and playing that trumpet until he was in high school, at which time, I purchased a brand new Bach Stradivarius, golden horn and hard-case, which he still occasionally plays, even today. Dana began marching with the Green Berets from the Holy Rosary Church in Lawrence. Angela had become a baton twirler and a majorette with the Alice Franz Dancers; sometimes both of our kids were marching in the same parade. Jet and I loved going to parades and marching band competitions, so this was right up our alley.

Dana came home from the Storrow Park playground, one day, and told his Mom that he wanted to get ice skates and learn to play hockey. She told him, "No way, you'll get killed!" He pleaded his case to me and I went right out and bought him a pair of ice skates and a hockey stick. It wasn't very long before I signed him up in the Lawrence Youth Hockey Program. They skated at the Frost Arena and now I was on the hook for skates, gloves, shoulder pads, helmet etc., but it was worth it. I never learned to ice skate or to play hockey. I used to ski in the winter when I was a kid, so this was a whole new world for me. We learned all about hockey together and he continued to play youth hockey until he graduated from high school. But it all started at Storrow Park on Prospect Hill when he was in the fourth grade.

Angela was becoming a very good Tap and Ballet Dancer. Jet and I went to all her recitals and special performances. She became a Student Teacher, helping Alice Franz with the little kids at the school. Angela obtained her license to teach tap, ballet and modern jazz and, at one time, thought she would like to open her own studio.

While living at Grace Terrace we had our first and only "breakup." I cannot honestly remember now what caused us to separate. It was an issue over some silly thing and I left, in a huff. I went back to my house on Tenney Street and began to stay there by myself. I did not call her; she did not call me. After a couple of weeks of this lonely life, I began to go out by myself to the movies, bars and visiting friends. One Friday night, Jet decided to go out and look for me to confront me. She put Dana to bed, got Sharon DuBois, her downstairs neighbor to keep an eye on him and called a taxi to take her to Tenney Street. I was not at home. She decided to continue looking for me. She knew that I hung out at the English Social Club over on Hampshire Street, about 10 blocks away.

She was not sure how to get there; having dismissed her cab and there were no cell phones then. So, she decided to walk to the club without a clue where it was located or even if I would be there. As luck would have it, she walked in the right direction and somehow found the place. She walked in and there I was sitting at the end of the bar, watching the floor show. She saw me right away, but I was looking in the opposite direction; I did not see her come in. She expected to see me with someone else, I think. She came up behind me and said something like,

"You really are a stubborn son of a gun, aren't you?" And I said, "Yes, I am." I was so happy to see her; I helped her up on an empty bar stool beside me; gave her a hug and a kiss and bought her a drink. We ended up back at my house, where we spent the night after calling Sharon DuBois to let her know that she would not be coming home until morning. Many times over the ensuing years, we both often wondered what would have become of us had she not gone out looking for me that night; or if she had not found me??

During the spring of 1973, I won the Engineering Excellence Award at the Merrimack Valley Works of Western Electric. This was a very prestigious award and only the second year that the award was ever presented, making me one of the first winners. The official presentation was made at the Andover Country Club at a formal dinner party.

Of course, Georgette accompanied me. I took her to Cherry & Webbs in Lawrence and bought her a beautiful, new gown for the occasion. We went, also to her hair dresser for a special hair style making her the most beautiful lady in the room. Lou Salazar, the Emcee for the event, announced our entrance. He presented us as, "Mr. Eddie Biron and his beautiful, Georgette." We had not yet married, so he was unable to present us as "Mr. & Mrs."

Following is the actual citation as it was presented on that occasion.

The Patent mentioned in the Citation is:

U.S. Patent No. 3,575,673 Date Issued: April 20, 1971
Entitled: Systems for Pulse Modulating a Signal

The WECo "The Engineer" article mentioned in the Citation was dated, January 1972 Volume XVI, Number 1. The Engineer was circulated internationally in those days; I received correspondence from the Post Master General in Helsinki, Finland, concerning my Time Domain article.

A New Development Letter for an ITE-5349 Waveguide TDR Test Set was Issued by E.J. Biron, February 22, 1972

MERRIMACK VALLEY WORKS

ENGINEERING
EXCELLENCE
PROGRAM

CITATION

Without a doubt, an award winner must have technical ability, awareness, and leadership. All of these should be coupled to good attitude and willingness to devote long hours to bring every project to a successful end. That is what has been said and written many, many times about this award winner.

Our man, not only proves his ability and leadership when summoned to the field, by "gently" but firmly guiding everyone connected with a trouble system, but also at the Merrimack Valley Works where he shines for his accomplishments. A few examples will suffice to clearly indicate the impact he has fostered upon the MV Works.

His numerous publications include an article for the "Western Electric Engineer" concerning his Time Domain Reflectometry Technique. And to show his versatility, he also designed the front cover for that issue.

His publications and technical literature have been designed to acquaint, describe and instruct. These have been of great help to those who have to work with the projects assigned to him.

He received a "Silver Medal" award for co-sponsoring an outstanding paper at the 11th Test Engineering Conference in Omaha, Nebraska.

He has a reputation for solving the diversified problems affecting our equipment when interfaced, here and in the field, with other manufacturers equipment.

Keeping alert for innovation, he is joint owner of the U.S. Patent entitled:

"System for Pulse Modulating a Signal."

This self-made man is never satisfied with mediocre performance. He is never hampered by the thought of ***"It Can't Be Done"*** or ***"It Can't Be Fixed."*** He is indeed a very determined man for a job well done. Perhaps a more meaningful tribute can be summed up by a poem written by a Mountain-Northwest Engineer pertaining to a system which for some reason could not be made to work.

Perhaps a more meaningful tribute can be summed up by a poem written by a Mountain-Northwest Engineer pertaining to a system which for some reason could not be made to work.

The last four lines simply state:

> Hours became days and days became weeks of dilly and dally,
> Someone suggests: Let's place a call to Merrimack Valley,
> The call is made under duress.
> An ***Associate*** came and cleaned up our mess…

Mr. Hilder—That Engineering Associate is our award winner—Ed Biron

The following poem was written by a guy named, Gerry DeRose, who worked for Western Electric in the Mountain Northwestern Regional Office in Aurora, Colorado. We never met one another. He sat in an office and week after week and month after month listening to telephone calls between engineers in his office and my office in the MV Works.

This poem is his interpretation of what went on out there in the field as a result of all these telephone calls he overheard.

TURNKEY—The SILENT SERVICE— by G. J. DeRose (1972)

The tower was up—The antennas hung,
New waveguide simmered in the noon day sun,
Inside the shelter, there was feverish preparation
As the installers finished the radio installation.
With a great deal of pride, as all could see,
A button was pushed to turn on the AC,
Then attention was turned to the lights on the tower,
All looked well, for there was power.

The work that remained to be done at this station,
Was the simple matter of antenna orientation.
The approaching car's course seemed to be erratic,
But it caused the crew to become ecstatic,

For although the job seemed very hectic,
In the car was the test man from Western Electric.
The installers heaved a sigh of relief,
But were unaware it meant more grief.

Now said the installer as he took the BSP,
"This station will be completed by the man from Turnkey,"
Long into the night as it started to rain,
They began to realize there was no gain.
All through the next day they were busy as bees,
They still had not increased the low DB's.
"I don't know what's the matter," said the test man in disgust,
"I'll bet the waveguide is all full of rust."

Apart came the waveguide piece by piece,
You see, they were looking for globs of grease.
They checked and rechecked all types of information,
Still the "voice with a smile" was silent at this station.

The antennas were moved in every direction,
Days became weeks of dilly and dally,
Then they placed a call to Merrimack Valley,
The call, as you know, was made under duress,
Then Eddie Biron came out and cleaned up the mess.

In 1973, while we were living on Grace Terrace in Lawrence, Georgette's oldest son, Billy, lost his wife, Jeanette to Lupis at only 28 years of age. She had been ill for a long time and she was aware of her terminal illness, but most of the family had no idea. She passed away at the Mary Hitchcock Hospital in Hanover, N.H. which is part of Dartmouth College. Jeanette knew that she would not enjoy a long life and so at Christmas time before she died; she made a special gift from ceramic for everyone in the family. For me, she made a beautiful, ceramic chess set; for Georgette, a two piece Christmas tree; and for Dana, a ceramic lamp with a figure of Bobby Orr #4 as a base.

We were driving to the hospital on a daily basis and Billy got himself temporarily transferred from the Hampton Beach fire station to the one in Hanover, so he could be close to Jeanette. The last time I saw her alive, she called me back as I was leaving her hospital room and asked me to give her a goodbye kiss. On the way back home, I told Georgette that we would not see her alive again. Sure enough, she passed away the next day on March 21st, 1973.

William (Little Bit), their only son, was about 4 years old at the time. With his mother gone and his father working a very heavy schedule, our grandson was spending a great deal of time with a sitter who lived up the street. Georgette and I offered to take the boy to live with us, where we intended to raise the two boys (Dana and William) together. I had already purchased bunk beds, so they could share a bedroom. Billy did not accept our offer. He said, "I don't want my son going to school in Lawrence." That was certainly a valid concern, at the time. The Lawrence school system was not very highly regarded. I did not intend to adopt either boy or to change their name or identity in any way. We were only attempting to ensure both boys a loving and secure environment while receiving a good education.

The ceramic chess set that Jeanette made for me as a Christmas gift in December, 1972, deserves a more elaborate description. The pieces were made of pure black and white, glazed ceramic; the King and Queen were at least 4 ½ to 5 inches high and measured 2 inches in diameter at the base. These pieces were obviously much too large to be used on an ordinary Checker/Chess Board. When my friend, Ernie Fusi, first saw the set of chess pieces, he offered to design and construct a special chess board upon which this particular set could be used. Ernie was a fellow Engineer at WECo and a good friend with whom I often played chess. The board that he came up with was a beautiful piece of workmanship; approximately 30 inches square; made with specially chosen wood that was inlaid in the correct pattern and highly polished. It was truly a work of art! I used it a few times, when I realized that the board was large and solid enough to become a table top. So I added the hardware necessary to attach four legs. It could then be used as both a board or a table. That table with the ceramic pieces in place became the "showpiece" everywhere we lived after that. The ceramic Christmas tree that Jeanette made for Jet was somewhat cumbersome and difficult to move around. The upper section of that tree found a place in our Florida home where we lit it up every Christmas until 2011, when we sold the house and moved back to Hampton Beach.

On November 1, 1974, I was promoted from Engineering Associate (EA) to Planning Engineer. There had been a friendly competition going on between Herbie Witherell and I; we were both EAs in the same group, sitting in the same cubicle; but we were assigned to different responsibilities. We were also the two highest paid EAs at the Merrimack Valley Works. Herbie was attending college at Northeastern in Boston 3 nights a week, year round; on the company's Tuition Refund Program to obtain an Engineering Degree that would enhance his chance for promotion. I, on the other hand, was traveling all over the country, 2 or 3 weeks each month; "putting out the fires" that kept cropping up. I was hoping to get promoted by hard work and good performance. Early on, I told Herbie, "You take the high road and I'll take the low road and I'll get to the next level before you." Actually, Herbie was promoted to Planning Engineer just one re-rate period before me. Ironically, the very same thing occurred when we were promoted to Senior Engineer a few years later; Herbie moved up to Senior Engineer and the very next re-rate period, I moved up, as well.

By this time, I had become a very proficient system trouble shooter. Whenever projects got in serious trouble, behind schedule, over budget, and everyone associated with them were pointing fingers at each other for the blame; I was called upon to come up with the solution. When I arrived on the scene; all the easy fixes had been attempted and a great deal of time and expense had gone down the tubes. I had nowhere to go but up and I was never afraid to fail. I had developed an uncanny ability to find someone or something that everyone else had missed. I also had a great deal of experience and a fantastic memory to assist with achieving success every time. I had no competition among my peers; no one else in my group would volunteer for the real complex problems because they were simply afraid of failure. Another asset that I possess, is unusual powers of observation. I could sometimes merely look things over visually and spot something unusual or abnormal. My next story will clearly demonstrate that particular ability and it is only one of many I could tell. One day, I was sent to Kentucky to help solve some very confusing issues. The problem came about as a result of installing a new microwave radio system "picky back" on top of an older system which had been performing pretty well before. It seems shortly after the second system was installed, both systems were performing poorly. There was a great deal of noise and crosstalk on the telephone circuits up and down the route. Taking a folder containing information about that route and system configuration with me, I boarded a plane from Boston's Logan Airport to Lexington, Kentucky; where I rented a car and headed for Middlesboro to meet a man named, Leroy Crow, "with an "e"; ergo, Crowe!! As soon as we met, I climbed into his pickup, and headed up the mountain to the first repeater site out of Middlesboro. As we were winding our way up the mountain, I asked Leroy to stop the pickup, and said, "I think I see the problem here." "No way," says Leroy. I said to him very confidently, "Yeh, way!" We disembarked from the truck and I pointed to the top of the hill and asked him, "Is that tower located on the site we're heading for?" "You bet," he responds. I asked, "Do you see anything unusual up there?" "Nope," he says.

Then I said to him, "Look closely and you will see that the top, 20 foot section of that tower is way out of plumb. One of the 3 guy wires that support that section has no tension and is hanging loosely to the ground. The three reflectors mounted on top appear to be oriented incorrectly." Then, we got back into the pickup and I went on to say, "When we get up there, I will explain exactly what happened and how we are going to fix it." When we arrived at the top of the mountain,

I could tell immediately that a strong wind, maybe a tornado, had struck the antennas mounted on top of the tower, twisting them out of alignment and pulling the anchor bolt, concrete and all, out of the ground to which the loose guy wire was attached. I got on the phone in the shelter under the tower and called the best sub-contract, tower crew in the country; Vulcan Construction from Indiana. The next morning, the crew arrived on site prepared to plumb the tower, re-tension the guy wires and orient the antennas. They came equipped with foul weather gear, walkie talkies, a transit, plumbing grid, come alongs etc. Everything that I had ordered the night before. To make things difficult, a snow squall came up in the middle of our plumbing procedure, making it hard to see the plumbing grid. In order to maintain telephone service, we plumbed the tower by tensioning the guy wires very slowing while simultaneously adjusting the antennas for maximum signal strength. I don't think anyone had ever done this before. I ran the whole show inside the hut at the base of the tower. I maintained communication with everyone involved by walkie talkie, while monitoring the signal strength meters and other instruments. The point here is that I saw the problem before I ever got to it.

Here is another true story to demonstrate my ability to find a person who has valid data or information leading me to the solution of the problem, but are unaware of it. Ironically, this project was also located in Kentucky. This project dealt with Cable Television (CATV) for the State of Kentucky. The head end was in Lexington and the tail end at Hazard. They were having difficulty meeting the Video System Requirements from end to end. From the top of the mountain at Hazard, one can see into 3 states; Virginia, North Carolina and Tennessee. Again, I flew from Boston to Lexington, Kentucky; rented a car and drove to a mountain top hotel near Dogpatch, appropriately called, "The Citadel." Here I met a motley crew of craftsmen and installers who had been working this project for over 3 months. They were thinking, "What is this guy going to do for us? Who does he think he is anyway?" I wasn't really sure what my first move was going to be. I scanned the room looking for I didn't know what. I spotted this young fellow camped over by the fireplace sucking up some heat. He appeared to be bored by the whole scene. I spoke to him, saying, "Hey, son, how long has it been since you've been home?" "Over 3 months, Sir," was his reply. I asked him if he had worked the route all the way down from Lexington and he said that he had. Then I asked him where he thought the trouble was. He looked at me as if I was crazy. Nobody had ever asked him what he thought about anything before. He thought about my question for a minute and then, he said, "I think something is wrong at Bledsoe." I asked him why he thought the problem was located there. His response was, "Things went well each time we came down the route, until we got to Bledsoe. Antenna orientation went well until we got there; in-place testing, video testing, system testing; same thing, everything went haywire at Bledsoe." Many of the crew members began to nod in agreement once it was called to their attention. I was now convinced that the problem was at the Bledsoe Repeater site. I divided the crew into 3 test groups; one team was to go to the site prior to Bledsoe with the test equipment that I prescribed, another to the site located after Bledsoe with the same equipment and I was headed to Bledsoe with the remainder of the crew. We met on the order wire at 0800 the next morning. I ran a battery of tests between the sites and in less than an hour, I located the problem, made the necessary repairs and was on my way home.

Over the years, I came to learn that sometimes all I had to do was to ask the right people the right questions.

Another characteristic that I possess; I am the classic opportunist, just let me get my foot in the door and I end up running the place. I have been that way all of my life. Look at what happened at Western Electric; when they waived the two year college requirement for me and opened the doors of the engineering world to me, I took full advantage of my golden opportunity and went as far as I could go.

In the late 1970's, I became a member of the Western Electric Speakers Bureau. Established in 1966, the speakers bureau offered speakers, free of charge, to civic organizations, church groups, clubs and educational facilities. It's purpose was to provide a good will service to communities in which the Western Electric operated. Besides being called upon to talk to various groups on a variety of subjects, I was also expected to be a good-will ambassador for the telephone company and a representative for "Ma Bell." I was sent to headquarters in New York City for special training. They did not teach me very much about public speaking, but they did teach me about being an ambassador for the company. I was always a very good story teller. They taught me things like; not to jingle the change in my pocket when speaking to a group and to maintain eye contact with some people in the audience. The talks consisted of a "canned" show with slides and a script. I usually changed some of the slides to update the information and provide better coverage of the subject matter and I modified the script to better suit my own style and delivery. I spoke on many subjects, as requested, from a list provided by the bureau to the public. My two favorite talks were: one on "Solar Energy" and another on the "Metric Connection." I gave those talks to many groups in the area; such as, the Moose, Elks, Rotary and Kiwanis.

I was also privileged to speak at various Salvation Army locations, as well as, very small groups, like; a small group of ladies who called themselves "Friends of the Georgetown (MA) Public Library." Having become so popular around the Merrimack Valley, these organizations would ask for me by name, even though there were other speakers available at our plant. A "spinoff" from my Speakers Bureau activity; I became active in the "Career Day" program being offered at many of the local high schools. I began talking to high school students about: "Careers in Engineering." Speaking to high school students about a career in engineering without the benefit of a college education was a challenge for me. Never advocating that it was the way for them go, I could not suggest that they rule it out either. After all, college was not on the agenda for many of these kids. Because of my own experience, however, I was able to provide them with some good information. One of my favorite areas of advice was to stress the development of good communication skills. Over the years, I learned that very intelligent people often have difficulty exchanging their ideas.

The academic requirements for future engineers are well established; the required math and science etc. Communication skills are often overlooked. I strongly urge all young people going on to college to take the following elective subjects: one, a course in public speaking, two, a course in technical writing, and three, a course in mechanical drawing (drafting). Some of these may be offered in high school; take them if offered, is my advice. These three subjects will provide them with the skills necessary to write about, to talk about and to draw a picture of any new ideas or inventions they may come up with. I explained to my listeners that I was able to take advantage of only one of these electives in high school; I took 2 years of Mechanical Drawing. I was forced to develop the other two on my own time. I got very good at writing and speaking. In fact, I became the "editor" for my engineering department, over time. I would "blue pencil" all the memos, trip reports and expense vouchers that were generated by my entire engineering department; checking for spelling, grammar and punctuation.

CHAPTER 19

"Our Day Will Come"

By this time, my first wife, Penny, and Georgette had become good friends; there was no hard feelings between them. In fact, at some point, Penny had suggested to Georgette to stick with me because, she said, "He has a big heart." It was about this time, my first wife, Penny, decided to divorce me. I did not contest the divorce; I had been unwilling to do it myself, however. There were no custody or support issues to contest. I continued to support Angela and Penny maintained her custody by mutual agreement.

After the appropriate "waiting period," required by the State of Massachusetts, Penny married Fred Lindner, and offered to buy me out of our mutually owned property on Tenney Street; so they could live there. So Georgette and I went house hunting in Salem, N.H., where Jet's brother, Arthur Fortin (Chippy), ran a real estate agency. We dealt with one of his female agents exclusively; seeking a brand new home. I had learned earlier that Jet would never agree to live in a home which someone else had already occupied. After a good deal of searching, we found a place we both liked on Glen Denin Drive in Salem. The next day, I called Harvey Ellis at the Merrimack Valley Credit Union and told him our plans. He cleared the deal over the telephone. Then I called Georgette and asked, "Do you really want that house we saw last night on Glen Denin Drive?" She answered, "Are you kidding me, of course?" "It's yours!" I said.

It was a brand new, 3 bedroom split level with a one stall garage under located on the corner of Townsend Avenue and Glen Denin Drive. It was a beautifully landscaped, corner lot, in the woods. I moved in there from Tenney Street; Georgette and Dana moved in from Grace Terrace on the same day in July, 1975. I hired a U-Haul truck; her 2 older boys helped me move from both locations to the new house. The builder, Donald Meisner, was asking $42,000; I offered $38,000, which he accepted in a heartbeat, the housing market was not doing well that year. I put $8000 down and paid the balance in less than a year. I also received a huge tax break, $3000 that year, for being a first time buyer of a new house that had not been offered for a lower price. That law was enacted as an incentive for prospective buyers to buy a new house that year; designed to help improve the housing market. I beat the first time buyer requirement because I bought the house jointly with Georgette; certainly the first time we purchased a house together. I actually paid only $35,000 for that house; 12 years later, it sold for $155,000. I paid no capital gains tax because the tax laws, were changed, in the meantime. We furnished and did a lot of interior decorating in that house. I also did some landscaping and worked on getting a good lawn started. Dana went into the 7th Grade at the Woodbury School in September. On November 8, 1975, Georgette and I were married in a civil ceremony in Salem, N.H. by a Lawyer and Justice of the Peace, Ralph Stein, who was a personal friend of Jet's brother Chippy. My brother, Buddy was my Best Man and, Georgette's sister, Bella, was the Maid of Honor. Our reception was held at the Ashworth Hotel in Hampton Beach with family and friends attending.

We spent 13 years on Glen Denin Drive, from 1975 to 1988. We became Band Parents, Hockey Parents, Dance Recital Parents and Jayvee Soccer Parents. I spent a great deal of time driving kids all over New England to football, soccer and hockey games. I enjoy telling the story about what happened to me one Saturday in the Fall of 1979. Dana and I arose at 4:00 A.M. and drove to the Skowhegan Skating Rink in Merrimack, N.H. for a 5:30 A.M. ice hockey practice session. There was no ice in Salem to skate on, in those days; we were forced to go elsewhere to get "ice time." After hockey practice, we headed back to Salem High School literally changing "on the fly" in the car for a 10:00 A.M. Salem Jayvee Soccer game. After the game, Dana showered and changed, at the school into his Salem High School Band uniform, which I had gone home to get while he was playing soccer. I also brought his hockey gear home at that time for laundering; we had a hockey game that evening. At 12:00 noon, he boarded the bus with the band at the high school and headed to Portsmouth, N.H. to play in the half-time show at the Salem High School Blue Devils versus the Portsmouth High School Clippers football game.

Before the game was over, I required permission to drive him home to Salem instead of waiting for the school bus because he had a hockey game to play that evening. Back home we go, eat supper, get back into his hockey gear that Mom had washed while we were at the football game. After supper, I drive Dana and two other kids, Scott DiPietro and Kevin Walley with all their hockey equipment; to Skate 3 in Tyngsboro, Ma. for a Salem N.H. Youth Hockey League game which starts at 8:00 P.M. We got back home to Glen Denin Drive about 11: P.M. that night. Talk about a long day at the office; this day started at 4:00 A.M. and ended at 11:00 P.M. This was probably the longest and most busy day of that period; there were many other days and nights that came close.

While living in Salem, Jet and I went to a great many parades and high school band competitions. We really enjoyed the half-time shows at the football games. In the parades, Dana would be playing the trumpet and marching with the Salem High School Blue Devils, and other times, Angela would be twirling her batons and marching with the Alice Franz Dancers. I would also take some of the other neighborhood kids to the parades with us.

In June 1976, Angela graduated from Castle Junior College in Windham, N.H., with an Associate's Degree in Business Science. That concluded 14 years of Catholic School Education for which she never forgave me; 8 years of elementary school at Saint Monica's in Methuen, 4 years of high school with the sisters at Saint Mary's in Lawrence and 2 years of junior college at Castle Junior College in Windham. Many years later, when she was dragging my granddaughter, Destiny, from Haverhill to Saint Augustine's parochial school in Andover on a daily basis; her reason was: "But Dad, I can't get a good public school education in this area for my child." My response: "Really! Seems like I heard that song before." It is certainly nice to know that the older we get, the smarter our children think we are. You know that you did something right, when you hear your children saying the same things to their children, that you said to them when they were young.

On July 4, 1976, the 200th birthday of this country, Angela married her first husband, Bob Taylor, at noon. Church bells were ringing from the steeples of every church in the land as I walked her down the aisle to give her away. She was married at the Advent Christian Church on Lowell Street in Lawrence; her Uncle Buddy was the presiding minister. I gave her a reception at Joe Binette's on Essex Street in Lawrence in the same building that once housed the Capri night club.

On January 1, 1984, Western Electric and the Bell Laboratories became an integral part of the American Telephone & Telegraph Company (AT&T) and all the operating companies (Baby Bell's) were combined into seven regional companies. I became an employee of AT&T until I retired in 1989. This came about because the famous Judge Greene and the Department of Justice, who had been trying to break the company up for a long time, declared that we were a monopoly. In other words, he tried to fix something that wasn't broken. The telephone business has never been the same since. I did get promoted to Senior Engineer on March 1st, 1984. Everyone seemed to agree, that making Western Electric, the Manufacturing and Installation part of the our business; Bell Laboratories, the Research and Development arm of the business; come under the umbrella of AT&T made a lot of sense. Investors were reminded that because the Bell Labs "think tank" employed 1500 PHDs, more than all the colleges and universities in the USA and possessed thousands of patents, that AT&T stock was a sound investment. Fact is, the stock did rise for a while; then it tanked!

Smoking had become a huge issue in our household in the 70's. Georgette became the last holdout in the family. None of our children or grandchildren are smokers. They were constantly begging her to quit. When Jet was 19 years old, working in the shipyard in Boston during World War II, she was already smoking 3 packs of cigarettes a day. When I met her, she was smoking more than one pack a day. As for me, I smoked just about everything one could possibly smoke from corn-silk when I was 12 years old to cigarettes, cigars and even a pipe when I was in the Navy. I never did smoke more than one pack a day nor did I ever smoke my first cigarette each day until I had something to eat. In the service, I was accustomed to seeing my shipmates rise in the morning and as soon as one foot hit the deck, they would light up their first smoke of the day. Most of my smoking was done after dinner or while "bending elbows" at a local pub. I actually quit smoking, "cold turkey," around 1965 or 1966; it was very close to the time that the Surgeon General ordered the tobacco companies to place a warning label on every package of cigarettes, alerting smokers of the hazards of smoking. What we did not know, at that time, was the damage done to our bodies from smoking is irreversible. That is, even if we quit smoking years later, the damage may have already occurred.

I did have one lapse, when I started to smoke again. I was not even aware of it happening. I had gone on a business trip to Winston Salem, N.C. where Western Electric had a plant on Lexington Road. I spent a week there and when I was about to return to the Merrimack Valley Works, there was an airplane strike. I elected to take the train instead. When I got home, Georgette accused me of smoking again because she spotted a package of Pall Mall (my old brand) cigarettes in my shirt pocket; with one cigarette missing. Somewhere on that train ride, I had subconsciously gone to a machine and purchased a pack of cigarettes and lit one of them up. Then, I must have placed the remainder of the pack in my shirt pocket where I normally kept them and forgot all about it. This is testimony to the fact that we are all creatures of habit. It never happened again; I don't remember it happening the first time!

After using many ploys aimed at encouraging Jet to quit smoking, I finally offered to buy her a house at the beach, if she would make a real serious effort to quit.

CHAPTER 20

"By the Sea"

"Jet's Rock"

She did agree and in March 1985, we purchased the front portion of a condex (2 unit condo) at Hampton Beach, N.H. on Kings Highway between 15th and 16th Streets. The beach house was actually located less than 300 feet from the high water mark at the seawall on Ocean Boulevard at 16th Street. This spot has been affectionately known as "Grampy's Beach" ever since. We owned the place at the beach from March 1985 until October 2011. When we retired on December 31, 1989; we began spending 6 months at the beach and 6 months at our home in Barefoot Bay, Florida. Soon we were staying 5 months in New Hampshire and 7 months in Florida. Finally, we gravitated to 4 months in the North and 8 months in the South. Georgette tried very hard to quit smoking, but occasionally she would sneak a smoke here and there. I knew it, but I did not let on that I was aware of it. One evening, when Dana came home from school in Boston, he spotted smoke wafting from the slightly opened bathroom window. He came running in to let me know. he said, "Dad, I think Mom is sneaking a smoke in the bathroom. I can see smoke coming from the window." I replied,

"I know, Son, don't say anything about it or she will start smoking out in the open again." "Let her think that she is putting something over on us. Give her a chance to beat this thing on her own."

Eventually, she did beat it. It took a few months, but she became one of the obnoxious ex-smokers. She got so that she could not tolerate the smell of smoke at all. When we were on the road and stopped at motels where they had converted some of their original rooms to "No Smoking" rooms, she could always tell, especially when they did a poor job of fumigating the rooms.

The entire family had some great times at Hampton Beach. There were fireworks, once a week all summer, fun in the arcades playing Skeeball and the concerts at the bandstand; were some of our favorite things. Swimming in the ocean and building sand castles. I would take the kids, toys, blankets and umbrella down on the sand. Nana (Georgette) would join us later with our lunch; goodies and drinks in a cooler. Every summer, we would have our grandchildren come and stay with us at "Grampy's Beach," a week or two at a time. I enjoyed having the kids come two at a time; but not two siblings. Siblings are always squabbling with one another and become very difficult to manage. I liked to invite, Tommy, our son George's number three son and Christal, Angela's daughter, stay with us at the same time because they were about the same age and they got along well together. I taught the kids how to body surf and how to ride the waves on "boogie boards." Our shed at the beach was full of things for kids and adults to play with: frisbies, badminton, dart board, pails and shovels, beach balls and surf boards. Flying a kite was always fun at the beach, as well. We had season tickets to the Hampton Playhouse summer theater for Wednesday matinees and our older grandchildren, Jason and Nicole enjoyed attending these shows with us.

During one of the very first summers that we spent at Hampton Beach, Jet and I threw the best party our family ever had. Those who came that are still alive, still talk about that party. Everybody came; we had to borrow picnic tables from our neighbors to make room for the huge gang that showed up. We had lobsters and a huge prime rib roast, fresh local NH corn-on-the-cob, iced cold beer and all the fixings. We made all the preparations and did all the cooking right there, on site. We had many other parties at the beach; but, we were never quite able re-create the atmosphere, enthusiasm and participation that came out of that event.

Georgette and I really loved living at shore, even in the off-season. One year, in late November or early December; it was raining and it was very cold at the beach. We walked along the seawall, all bundled up in warm clothing with rain slickers over us. We located a place to sit and watch the roaring ocean pounding on the shore, on a bench near the old Coast Guard Station. A photographer from the Hampton Union, our local newspaper, happened by and asked if he could take our picture for the next issue. We agreed and the photo appeared in a subsequent issue with the caption-"Diehard Beachgoers."

Before I retired from AT&T, I would often come home at the beach and find that Georgette was nowhere to be found. The sliding door that opened onto the deck would be open indicating that she had left the house a short time earlier. There was no cause for concern, however, because I always knew where she could be found. She had a favorite spot on the beach located at the 16th Street opening in the seawall. There was a large piece of granite rock which the winter tides and shifting sands had deposited there along the base of the wall. She would sit on that rock for hours looking out to sea; meditating and praying. It eventually became known as "Georgette's Rock." It is still there, but it can no longer be seen because the tides and shifting sands have buried it again. A few years ago, I placed her ashes in the ocean very close to "her rock."

Another favorite event living at the beach was to ride my bike down to the draw bridge between Hampton and Seabrook Beach in the early morning at high tide and watch the bridge go up to allow the party fishing boats go out to sea. The party boats with a high flying bridge and antennas have insufficient clearance to get under the bridge at high tide. The drawbridge, therefore, must be lifted to allow the traffic to pass under it. The drawbridge operator was a fellow named, Carl Furlong, who was a retired AT&T Engineer who worked with me. Carl was also an Engineering Excellence Award winner at the MV Works and he retired the same time as I did. Another bit of trivia about Carl Furlong: He played basketball for the Haverhill Boys Club 100 pounders back in the 1940's with my brother, Buddy; Bobby Wysocki, who became my Manager at AT&T and Carlo Braci, who was a Supervisor at AT&T in charge of a shop for which I once was the Product Engineer. It surely is a small world, isn't it?

Every Tuesday evening, I played chess with a group of men who lived in the area at the Hampton Public Library. I would drive Georgette to Seabrook to play Bingo at the old fire station there. Then I'd return to Hampton; play chess, returning to pick her up at a designated time and place and go on home together.

One day, our grandson, Little Bit pulled up at the beach house in a truck carrying some "hot top" on board and a crew to make some repairs on the surface of my two parking lots. He had previously told me that if he ever had some "hot top" left over from a job, he would come and repair my parking area with it instead of discarding the material on the way back to the shop. He was working for Charlie Maclaughlin paving driveways and parking lots, as well as, landscaping and lawn mowing; a position with very little future. I asked him to stop by and chat with me some day when he had the opportunity, so we could discuss his future.

A week or maybe two later, he returned and what ensued changed his life forever! We chatted at the kitchen table in the beach house; and I asked him, point blank, "William," I asked, "What do you want to be when you grow up?"

I was being facetious because he was about 20 years old at the time. He thought about my question for a considerable amount of time before uttering, "a Civil Engineer." My next question was, "What have you done so far to achieve that goal?" He proceeded to tell me; he had taken some courses at Northern Essex Community College in Haverhill and some courses at UNH in Durham, N.H. He had no idea how much credit he had already acquired or which schools would accept that credit toward their Civil Engineering Program. So, we developed a strategy aimed at reaching his goal. I advised him to meet with his guidance counselors at both schools, get a transcript of his grades to determine how much credit he may have already earned; then, find out which schools in the area would accept it. Little Bit did his home work and we learned that Umass at Lowell would accept most of his credits and that in 2 years, including Summer School, he could earn a Bachelor's Degree. I advised him to move from Seabrook, N.H. to Lowell, Mass. and establish residency there because UMass is a state university which offers reduced tuition rates for Mass. residents. Then, I suggested that he take a lease on a place large enough for one or maybe two room mates to help pay the rent and utilities. I agreed to co-sign a student loan, if he needed it, as well. I am not suggesting that William followed every one of my recommendations, but we certainly developed a good "game plan" together. Ultimately, he earned his degree and went immediately to work for Parini Construction and later with Welsh Brothers Engineering firm in Boston. He has been Project Manager on many of the new buildings on the Boston skyline. When William graduated from UMass Lowell, I struggled with the dilemma of a meaningful gift. I finally settled on the ceramic chess set that his Mom had made for me some 20 years earlier; including the special board/table that Ernie Fusi had designed and built for me.

During the Christmas/New Years season of 1988 and 1989, we drove down to Florida on a two pronged mission. One, to take a vacation and check out the various tourist attractions and; two, to locate a second home to serve us with winter quarters when I went into retirement. I was originally planning on retiring at 60 years of age and time was getting short. We had sold the house on Glen Denin Drive in Salem with a few difficulties. Our potential buyers got stiffed by a buyer for their home on Tower Hill in Lawrence because they had lied on their loan application. They had already made an $8000 deposit which I was not about to return. I was able to convince our buyers, a nice young couple with two young children, to float a "bridge loan" until their house was sold.

CHAPTER 21

"On Moonlight Bay"

I had contacted Goldie Souliotis at Barefoot Bay Realty with our price range and requirements for our new home; she was prepared to show us some new and used homes there. We stayed at Tiara-by-the Sea, a motel right on the ocean at Melbourne Beach which was owned and operated by our son, Billy and his second wife, Carla. We stayed in the "Presidential Suite," the best room in the house. After looking at 6 or 7 homes there in Barefoot Bay, we purchased a brand new, 2 bedroom, 2 bathrooms, manufactured Jacobson Home at 1205 Areca Drive. I made a down payment and returned in April with my recently purchased 1986 Ford 150 Pickup truck loaded to the gills with stuff for our new house; to close on the sale and to start furnishing it.

Our timing was perfect because in June, 1989, AT&T announced an early retirement program for Management Personnel. The company was attempting to remove 12,000 management employees from their rolls by the end of the year. The offer included a 5 year addition to my age, a 5 year increase to my years of service and a 15% kicker until I went on Social Security. This became the "5-5-15" Retirement Plan of 1989. I responded immediately by reporting to Personnel requesting my pension be calculated based on the new formula. I was to be severed as if I was 64 years old with 44 years of service. It surely looked good to me; the only requirement was that the prospective retiree must be gone by the end of the year; that is, by December 31, 1989. No problem! In November, at the Thanksgiving break, I drove my pickup truck with Georgette, her clothes and some new furniture down to Barefoot Bay and I flew back to New Hampshire from Melbourne

Airport. I got a ride to the airport from Jack Holbrook, one of my ex-Department Chiefs, who had already retired and was living there in Barefoot Bay. In December, my boss, Lenny Pelletier, came and asked me why I was still hanging around the office. He said. "Get out of here. Go to Florida for Christmas! I'll check you out officially on the 31st," I turned in my company "all works" pass, my AT&T credit card, etc. to him; cleaned out my desk and left in a cloud of dust.

I returned to Barefoot Bay, just before Christmas, in my second vehicle, an Oldsmobile Cutlass Sierra with "Little Bit" sharing the driving. He got a speeding ticket in Fayetteville, N.C. on Interstate #95. I was snoozing and he was driving. He was caught doing 80 MPH in a 60 MPH zone by a state cop hiding under an overpass with his radar scanner. Our radar detector sounded, as well, just as we came over the cop's hiding place. Too late! The ticket cost me about $85.00, I think, and a promise not to tell his father.

No one, not any of my family or friends thought that I would be able to just up and retire from my job. I was a "workaholic"; the first person in the office each day and the last one out. I took my work home with me. I would go to sleep at night with problems on my mind and wake up in the middle of the night with the solutions. But, I had begun preparing myself for retirement at least a year or so earlier and, of course, my wife was on board. I had already sold the house in Salem, NH and purchased a place in Florida; we planned to keep the house at Hampton Beach. I was in great shape; physically and financially; no debt of any kind. I planned on golfing a lot and traveling, especially traveling. We were both in reasonably good health and we were prepared for a new adventure. In spite of all that, the "Headhunters" were out there trying to get me back to work. Of course, they could get me at a much cheaper rate because employers were no longer required to provide any benefits: such as, paid holidays or vacations, health benefits or sick days. I was finally able to get them off my back by continually refusing their offers. If I wanted to continue working, I would not have retired in the first place. No employer could have duplicated the rate of pay and the benefit package that I was enjoying, when I retired.

In the first 10 years of retirement, we went on at least a dozen cruises; including a Mediterranean Cruise to Italy, Greece, Turkey, Monaco and Spain. We enjoyed 2 weeks each year for 10 years at Carnival time (Feb) in Aruba at an all-inclusive resort, called the Bushiri Resort. We also spent 2 weeks each year for 10 years in November at the Las Palmas Resort in Puerto Vallarta, Mexico. We stayed as guests of friends, Walt and Dottie Stiebitz, who owned a timeshare there. We occupied adjoining rooms with balconies which looked into the sunsets over Banderos Bay. We paid only for the round trip airfare from Florida each November and most of our meals.

In June 1995, Georgette and I took a 12 day cruise that took us to: Venice, Italy; Zakynthos, Greece; Kusadasi, Turkey; Athens, Greece; Naples, Italy: Rome, Italy; Florence, Italy; Cannes, France; Monte Carlo, Monaco; Majorca Island, Spain and Barcelona, Spain. This Mediterranean cruise turned out to be the greatest adventure of our retirement experience because it fulfilled a couple of lifetime dreams; to visit the Isle of Capri, which my mother often sang to me about as a child; and to throw coins while making a wish into the Trevi Fountain in Rome. Our trip started out with an overnight flight, First Class, from Boston to Rome via Al' Italia Airlines. Then a short flight, a puddle jumper, from Rome (It.-Roma) to Venice (It.-Venezia), where we picked up our cruise ship the "Pacific Princess," The ship was the original "Love Boat," the same one we all saw on TV for many years. Shortly after our trip, the Love Boat was sold to the Chinese, because it was too small to compete with the huge cruise ships that were being built at that time.

While in Venice we had the opportunity to spend two days and one night, visiting all the sights that we had heard and read about. In Venice, there are no cars or roadways, just canals and boats. Georgette and I got to ride in a gondola with a singing gondolier under the famous Bridge of Sighs. We fed the pigeons in Saint Marks Square, visited the Palace of the Doges, the Rialto Bridge, St. Marks

Basilica, saw the renowned Murano glass blowers and took a boat ride around the lagoon which surrounds Venice. Because I was able to speak conversational Italian quite well, the natives treated me as if I was one of them which made it easier to get directions and to bargain for better prices when shopping. I bargained and finally purchased six glass goblets with 24 Karat gold trim from the Murano glass blowers. They packed them in Styrofoam and shipped them to Hampton Beach, free of charge and guaranteed against breakage for three or four hundred thousand lire. Venice being the first port of call on the cruise, the Italian salesman also guaranteed that the goblets would get to Hampton before we got back. They did and none was broken either. Back then, they did not accept the Discover Card in Italy; I used my AT&T Universal Card and paid the bill in Italian lire because the credit card companies can obtain a better rate of exchange than I could get. When I finally paid the credit card company off in U.S. dollars, I figured that I paid about $35.00 apiece for those goblets. It was a very good deal at the time; gold was $35.00 an ounce. Today, gold is running between $1300 and $1500 an ounce! I distributed those goblets among the family, keeping one for myself. I still have it. I think the gondola ride was the high point of the cruise for Georgette and the one experience she remembered the most. Every time she saw scenes from Venice on TV and saw the gondolas, she would always cry out, "I've been there! Done that!"

The next port of call was, Zakynthos, a beautiful green island in Greece, surrounded by the clear, blue water of the Ionian Sea. The island is famous for its wide, sandy beaches where one can swim and snorkel in the company of sea turtles. We went ashore for a few hours there and found the people very friendly. I bought a magnificent, hand made fan for Georgette there. I still have it, as well.

We were at sea for 2 nights and a day before arriving at Kusadasi, Turkey. Kusadasi is a beach resort town on Turkey's Western Aegean coast and the jumping-off point for visiting the ancient city of Ephesus. We boarded a tour bus and headed for Ephesus where we spent the better part of a day, before returning to the ship. The House of the Virgin Mary turned out to be a grotto or a cave where it is said she lived out her last days. We visited the ruins of the Temple of Artemis, one of the Seven wonders of the ancient world and the Church of St. John. It was John who took Mary with him to Ephesus when it was a major seaport and trading center. Our guide was a young Turk lady, who was very knowledgeable in all the religions practiced in the area. She was educated in the Turkish city of Izmir, located a few miles away from Ephesus and spoke English very well. I asked her, "How did John and Mary get here from the Holy Land? Did they come overland on the backs of animals or did they come by sea?" She told me that no one knows for sure; since there are no records or documents. However, she believed they came by sea because Ephesus was a very popular and accessible sea port and overland travel was very difficult in ancient times. While riding the bus between Kusadasi and Ephesus, I noticed the presence of the Turkish military scattered all over the countryside, heavily armed and obviously ready for trouble. The area has always been a tinderbox of political unrest.

Another night at sea and we arrived in Piraeus, Greece, the seaport for Athens; about 25 miles away by bus. My first impression of Piraeus; it has to be the largest seaport in the world. At least, the largest that I had ever seen, including Hampton Roads near Norfolk, Va. which is huge! There were dozens of cruise ships from all over the world, some at anchor and many tied up at docks. There was a large number of oilers and freighters. Dozens of Men-of-War flying the colors of many nations of the world . Everywhere I looked, in all directions, as far as I could see, there were ships. I never saw so many ships in one place!

From the Love Boat, we boarded a tour bus right on the dock and headed for Athens. Automobile and bus traffic in Athens moves very slowly; the streets are very old and narrow. While we were there, many of the main streets were under repair in an attempt to widen and resurface them. This process became very slow because every time excavation began, relics were often uncovered. One could not begin to conceive what may lie beneath the streets of an ancient city like Athens. The work stopped and archeologists took over to recover and protect the artifacts that were found. Road traffic had to be delayed and/or rerouted. It was very hot when we arrived at the site of the Acropolis; about 90 degrees in the shade and there was no shade. The word "acropolis", in Greek, means a citadel, built on elevated ground. Georgette and I walked up to the very top of the high hill upon which the Acropolis of Athens was built. She was using her fold-away cane and we stopped and rested many times along the way. The view over the city below was incredible. The Parthenon is also located atop that hill. The Parthenon is a former temple dedicated to the goddess, Athena, whom the people of Athens considered their patron. It is the most important surviving building of Classical Greece, considered by many to be the zenith of the Doric order. The next site visited on the tour was the Panathinaiko Stadium, a 4th century BC stadium which was restored for the games in 1896.

Greece is where the Olympic Games began in the 11th century BC. When Athens won the right to hold the 2004 games, people wondered if the chaotic and polluted city could make it work; they did, resulting in a rebuilding program which re-vitalized the city.

A couple of days later, we dropped anchor in the Bay of Naples (It.-Napoli), where we were given a choice of three tours to take from the ship; 1st—a tour of the ruins at Mt. Vesuvius; 2nd—a tour of the Amalfi Coast, and 3rd-a visit to the Isle of Capri. That's the one I wanted, Capri! The first thing in the morning, we caught a motor launch from our cruise ship to a dock in the harbor at Sorrento and walked over two docks and boarded a hydrofoil to Capri. A hydrofoil is a boat that has fins attached to the bottom by struts for lifting the hull clear of the water allowing much faster speeds. It was the first time we had ever seen such a boat, let alone taken a ride in one. Then a small bus took us from the water front at Marina Grande up the mountain to the Piazza Cimitaro near the top of the mountain. The very top of the mountain is called Anacapri and can only be reached on foot. Our guide, Guido, escorted us there to show us a magnificent view and some grandiose villas. The ride up the mountain was very scary, especially because I was seated in the window seat on the right side of the bus. I felt that, at any moment, we would go over the edge into the sea, far below. The road is narrow, winding its way up the hill very close to the edge of sharp, picturesque cliffs. The drivers never slow down on the sharp curves; never apply the brakes, they just keep pounding on the horn. Vehicles coming down in the other lane were doing the same thing. We ate lunch around noon at a quaint Italian restorante located just off the Piazza Cimitaro. It was a typical Italian pasta dish with wine and all the trimmings. We dined "al fresco" (outdoors) under a ceiling of the most beautiful Bougainvillea I have ever seen. We came down the mountain by way of the Funiculare, which is a cable railway running through a tunnel down the mountain to the marina. We returned to the Love Boat exactly the same way we had come. We enjoyed the entire tour for one price; the guide, all transportation, refreshments along the way and lunch on the island. Everything except for whatever souvenirs we may have purchased along the way. I fulfilled a dream of a lifetime.

I also experienced two minor disappointments. We were unable to do the Blue Grotto tour because the seas were unusually high that day and I was also unable to find a jewelry or music box that plays the song, "On the Isle of Capri." From the moment I arrived on Capri until the time I boarded the hydrofoil to return to Sorrento, I browsed every souvenir shop and novelty store looking for anything that played that song. I almost lost my tour party a couple of times when I strayed away from them while searching. There has always been some controversy about the lyrics to that song; do the lyrics refer to an apple tree or a walnut tree or whatever? My Mom always sang the second line: "In the shade of an old ***walnut*** tree." I asked Guido, our guide, about it and he told me there are no walnut trees on Capri, or apple trees for that matter. He told me that the song must have been written by an Americano stupido (stupid American) who had never been to Capri. Sometime later, I heard Bing Crosby and Rosemary Clooney singing that song on my car FM radio from the sound track of an old 78 RPM, monaural, vinyl record. Bing, Rosemary and my Mom all agreed; it's a walnut tree.

Next port of call was, Civitavecchia, the port for Rome (It.-Roma). We signed up for another complete tour because it had worked out so well for us in Naples. We boarded a bus on the dock and arrived in Rome about an hour and a half later. From that bus we visited the Vatican, the Sistine Chapel, St. Peters Basilica, the Coliseum, Fountain of Trevi, and had dinner in a famous Italian restaurant; not necessarily in that order. Our first stop was the Sistine Chapel, the Apostolic Palace, the official residence of the Pope in Vatican City. The chapel was built between 1477 and 1480 by Pope Sixtus IV, for whom it is named. The ceiling in the Sistine Chapel which contains Michelangelo's Frescoes, has to be one of the most extraordinary pieces of art in the world. It took him 4 years, from 1508 to 1512, working on a scaffolding, to complete the frescoes on the ceiling of the chapel. Looking up, I became truly captivated by the workmanship, beauty and colors of the scenes depicted there. There are 9 scenes from the Book of Genesis, 12 Prophetic Figures, 4 Pendatives and the ancestors of Christ displayed there. Restoration work had been completed on the ceiling a couple of years before I arrived, which made the colors appear fresh and spring-like with pale pink and sky blue against a background of warm grey. The frescoes had become discolored, over the years, by candle smoke making the pictures seem monochrome. The restoration removed the filter of grime to reveal the richness of the colors again. The work was met with both praise and criticism. Critics assert that much of Michelangelo's original work was lost in the removal of various accretions. Not having seen the frescoes prior to the cleaning process, I was unable to make any criticism. I only know that what I saw on that ceiling was "wicked awesome." To quote someone whose name I do not remember, "Without having seen the Sistine Chapel, one can form no appreciable idea of what one man is capable of achieving."

The bus stopped and parked at the Colosseum, where we disembarked and entered the huge amphitheatre with our tour guide. The Colosseum, also known as Flavian's Amphitheatre, was a very impressive site considering it was constructed in 70 AD. It took 10 years to complete and it was designed to hold 75,000 people. The thing that impressed me most was the manner in which the entrances and exits were designed; allowing them to evacuate the entire amphitheatre in 15 minutes; an engineering fete, even today. In the ruins, can be found the remains of toilet facilities for the throngs of attendees. It was here that the gladiators fought wild animals; such as, lions before huge crowds. The gladiators, who were mostly slaves or criminals, were often forced to fight each other to the death for the entertainment of the crowds. Sitting high up in the stadium and looking down into the arena below, I could almost sense the atmosphere that existed here during the games. Next stop, the Trevi Fountain (It.-Fontana di Trevi), scene of Anita Ekberg's dip in the movie La Dolce Vita (Eng.-The Sweet Life) is a flamboyant baroque ensemble of mythical figures and wild horses, which take up the entire side of the 17th Century Palazzo Poli. A recent restoration finished in 2015, has made the fountain gleam brighter than ever. Tradition is to toss a coin into the water, thus ensuring that you'll return some day to Rome. I threw two coins into the water, one for me and one for Georgette. I haven't returned, yet....but I have often thought about going back. It was in front of the Trevi Fountain where I engaged a vendor in an attempt to make a deal for some silver coins, similar to the U.S. Silver Dollar, depicting the images of the 19th Century Popes. After tossing my coins in the fountain, I began browsing among the wares on display by the vendors working the crowd. A set of these silver coins caught my attention; I picked them up and went to the vendor, and said, "Quanto costa?" (How much?) He looked at me, smiled and said, "Aspetta!" (Wait!) Then he went on in Italian to inform me that the set I was holding was incomplete; he disappeared behind his display and returned with another set of coins which he explained to me was the complete set in brillant, uncalculated condition. I asked again, "Quanto costa questo che?" (How much for this one?) He explained, still speaking Italian, that he was going to give me the complete set for the same price as the incomplete set. I said, it was a "Costa troppo." (It costs too much.) We finally settled for about 200 thousand Lira, which was about U.S. $26.00. I still have that set of silver coins.

It was a good buy then and still is. Once the vendor realized I spoke Italian, even though I was an American, he began to bargain more fairly with me. Next was Saint Peter's Square and Basilica. St. Peter's Basilica is the holiest place in Christendom, heart of the Catholic Church. Saint Peter is believed to have been buried there in 64 AD. The moment I walked into the basilica, I was so overcome by the solemnity of the place, I began to weep. The feeling of being in the presence of God, the Holy Father and all the saints is so overpowering, it is very difficult to describe. I was also impressed with its size and grandeur. There are over 60 sites to view within the basilica, such as; statues, monuments, altars, chapels etc. Our first stop, just inside on the right is Michelangelo's Pieta. I had first seen the Pieta in 1964 at the New York Worlds Fair in Flushing Meadows. The statue was on display under soft blue lighting which enhanced the pure white marble image. Viewers were forced to stand on a slowly moving, horizontal escalator as they passed by the display which was necessary to keep the large crowds moving along. Here in Rome, in a niche in St. Peter's Basilica, the Pieta seemed to be more at home. Outside the basilica, in the center of Saint Peter's Square, stands a tall, magnificent, Egyptian obelisk made of red granite. It is 41 meters high, to the cross at the top. It had been moved from Alexandria in 1586 and re-erected there in the center of the square. Pope John Paul II waved from a second story window in his quarters, to the crowd as we passed by; he was not well enough to receive visitors that day. We also had a delicious, Italian meal, served to us in a restaurant located somewhere along the route of our tour. When I entered the men's rest room to clean up before dinner, I noticed a portion of the floor was made of clear, blocks of glass. The building had been built over one of the ancient catacombs of Rome, which could be seen through the flooring. Further investigation revealed that many of the ancient burial grounds were uncovered during modern day construction activity. The tour bus returned us to our cruise ship as the crew was preparing to sail for our next port-of-call; an exhausted but fully enriched group of people.

The next morning, the Pacific Princess arrived at the Port of Leghorn (It.-Livorno), the port serving Florence (It.-Firenza). Again, we signed up for an all inclusive bus tour covering the Leaning Tower of Pisa, as well as, many of the sight seeing attractions in the Florence area. Florence is the capital of Italy's Tuscany region; birthplace of the Italian Renaissance and the home to many masterpieces of art and architecture. The first leg of our tour took us to the famous Leaning Tower of Pisa, which is the campanile (Eng.-bell tower) of the Cathedral of Pisa, known worldwide for its unintended tilt.

It is situated behind the Cathedral and Baptistry of Pisa in the Piazza dei Miracoli (Eng.-Miracle Square), formerly known as the Piazza del Duomo (Eng.-Cathedral Square). The tower is 183 feet high from the ground on the low side and 186 feet on the high side. The tilting of the tower was caused by an inadequate foundation on ground too soft on one side to properly support the weight of the structure. Many efforts were made to prevent the tower from more tilting by strengthening and stabilizing it. I was very disappointed with what I saw there. The tower was literally covered with ladders and scaffolding which made picture taking rather ludicrous. The tower was undergoing gradual surface restoration, in order to repair visible damage from corrosion and blackening caused by years of exposure to wind and rain. The cathedral (It.-Duomo), which dominates the Square of Miracles (It.-Piazza di Miracoli) is a masterpiece of architecture, however. with a magnificent facade of grey marble and white stone set with discs of colored marble. The massive bronze main doors are very impressive and the interior is faced with black and white marble, has a gilded ceiling and a frescoed dome. There are Corinthian columns of granite between the nave and the aisles. Galileo is believed to have formulated his theory about the movement of the pendulum by watching the swinging of the incense lamp (not the present one) hanging from the ceiling of the nave. Leaving Pisa and heading back to Florence, we passed row upon row of olive trees until we came to the town of Luca. As we approached Luca, I saw a large building off to the right, in the valley, with a large sign upon it, reading: "Berio." I thought; this must be where the olive oil comes from, that we buy at Hannafords and Market Basket. I remembered the labels on big cans of Berio olive oil, which read: "Imported from Luca, Toscano, Italia." Yep, this is it, that's exactly where we are! I would have liked to stop there for a tour, but our very busy schedule did not include a stop in Luca.

Back in Florence, we went to the Basilica di Santa Croce (Eng.-Holy Cross Cathedral), a massive Franciscan basilica with a facade enlivened by varying shades of colored marble. Most visitors come to see the tombs of Galileo, Michelangelo, Dante Alighieri and Ghiberti buried inside the church. It's frescoes by Giotti and his school in the chapels to the right of the main altar were the real highlights of this tour. There are a few relics of Saint Francis on display, including his cowl and belt. In the church bookshop, there is access to the Scuola del Cuoio, a leather school where I saw bags being fashioned which were also available for purchase.

Next, we visited Florence's Duomo (It.-cathedral), which is the city's most iconic landmark. Capped by a red-tiled cupola, it is constructed with a breathtaking pink, white and green marble façade and a graceful bell tower (It.-campanile) which dominates the medieval city. Inside, we saw frescoes by Vasari and Zuccari and at least 44 colorful stained, glass windows. The cathedral's cupola is one of the masterpieces of the Renaissance and is a feat of engineering which, they say, cannot be fully appreciated without climbing the 463 interior stone steps. We did not climb the spiral staircase because there was insufficient time and also because it was very steep and I did not believe that we were physically able. The Ponte Vecchio (Eng.-Old Bridge), is a Medieval, stone closed bridge over the Arno River which flows through the city of Florence. It has 3 arches and our short visit there revealed a host of shops and merchants who display their goods in front of their premises. I remember that we did not purchase anything there. We also stopped for a short visit at the Palazzo Vecchio (Eng.-Old Palace), Florence's town hall; a solid cubical shaped building built of solid rusticated stonework, enhanced by a simple rectangular tower with a large, one-handed clock. The tower, which is not directly centered in the building, is 308 feet tall. The entire structure is the most unusually shaped building that I had seen in my travels, which made our stop even more interesting. We also visited the Galleria dell' Academia (Eng.-Academy Gallery), the home of Michelangelo's sculpture of David. The statue stands 14 feet tall and it took him 4 years to complete (1501-1504) and all of the work was done outdoors in all kinds of weather. The museum contains other sculptures by Michelangelo and a large number of Renaissance paintings by Botticelli, del Sarto, Pontorno etc. but the statue of David is definitely the featured attraction there. When we returned to the ship that evening, we tried to remember all that we had seen that day; it had been an extremely busy day.

Next, we sailed for the Cote d'Azur, the French Riviera, where we dropped anchor, off shore at Cannes. I went ashore without Georgette because she wasn't feeling well enough to accompany me after the exhausting time we had spent in Florence, the day before. I decided to take the Monaco-Monte Carlo Tour from the ship that day. It began with a boat ride from the ship to a boat landing in Cannes, where I joined a bus full of tourists with a guide heading for St. Nicholas Cathedral in the Principality of Monaco. The bus ride between Cannes and Monaco, along the French Riviera, is one of the most beautiful sights in the world. I toured the cathedral with the group, where we came upon the tomb of Grace Kelly, the American actress, who became the Princess of Monaco when she married Prince Rainier, the Prince of Monaco. She was killed in an automobile accident in September, 1982 with her daughter, Stephanie in the car. After the cathedral tour, I had lunch on a second level terrace of a restaurant which overlooked the entrance to the casino at Monte Carlo. The Casino de Monte-Carlo is a gambling and entertainment complex, which includes, a casino, the Grand Theatre de Monte Carlo and the office of Les Ballets de Monte Carlo. The building has a beautiful, greenish blue dome and twin towers, which faces a huge mall of trees, gardens, fountains and pools.

Upon entering the casino, I was required to check my hat and camera and I was not permitted to wear clothing with words of any language printed on them; such as, "Boston Red Sox." Good thing that I was wearing a nice, colorful sport shirt. I went, immediately to a cashier and converted US $100 to Monaco francs. I played some slot machines and Black Jack. I did pretty well because I had a couple pockets full of the Monaco francs. I had to keep my eye on the clock because the tour bus back to Cannes was scheduled to pick us up in front of the casino at 3:00 PM. At about 2:45 PM, I went back to the same cashier to convert my money back to US dollars. They refused to give me my American money back to me! They said that I had to go to a bank to do that. "Ridiculous," I said. I told them that I was leaving the country in a few minutes never to return and that I would have no use for the Monaco money. I went to check out; picked up my hat and camera and proceeded to the door, where I asked one of the gendarmes guarding the entrance, where the nearest bank was located. He directed me to a side street up the mall a few hundred yards away and told me to hurry because the banks close at 3:00 PM in Monaco. I received about $180.00 in American money for the pockets full of francs that I had accumulated and the bank closed when I left. I dashed back to the casino just in time to catch the bus for Cannes. Had I missed that bus, I would have needed to hire a taxi at a premium price, I'm sure. I had fulfilled another dream of a lifetime, to play Black Jack at Monte Carlo, and won about $80.00 in the process. The bus arrived back in Cannes just in time to catch the last motor launch back to the Pacific Princess.

The next day we headed for Barcelona, Spain taking a route which brought us close enough to Majorca for a quick view. Majorca is an island in the Mediterranean Sea known for its beaches and sheltered coves, limestone mountains and Roman and Moorish ruins. Taking this route was intended to time our arrival in Barcelona with the departure of another Princess lines cruise ship, from the same pier. The bus trip from the port of Barcelona to the airport gave us a quick view of that very busy and crowded city. A TWA flight to New York's JFK

Airport connecting with another flight to Logan Airport in Boston, where we were met by family, who took us home to Hampton Beach.

We took eight other cruises over the first few years of my retirement. We visited islands in the Eastern and Western Caribbean, Mexico, Panama Canal, Bahamas and Bermuda. Four of those cruises started in San Juan, Puerto Rico. Five of them brought us to Saint Thomas in the U.S. Virgin Islands. We cruised to Nassau in Bermuda and to Cozumel, Mexico, twice. We also visited Ocho Rios in Jamaica, Cayman Islands, Grenada, and Saint Maarten, twice. Other islands visited on these cruises, in alphabetical order, are: Antigua, Barbados, Curacao, Dominica, Guadeloupe, Martinique, Saint Barts and Saint Lucia.

Here are some highlights from those eight cruises.

Our first cruise was a Western Caribbean cruise on the Carnival Cruise Lines, "Holiday" in November, 1991. It was touted as a Thanksgiving Holiday cruise on the MS Holiday. We went with Jack and Eileen Sousa, our neighbors from Salem, NH and fellow "Cursillistas." The Holiday sailed out of Miami, Florida, so we drove down from Barefoot Bay and the Sousa's flew down from Boston, to meet the ship. The highlight of that cruise was in Ocho Rios, Jamaica at Dunn's River Falls, where Jack and I swam down the falls and walked the stairway back up while the girls looked on.

We enjoyed three voyages on the MS Tropicale; one, in 1995, included a Panama Canal experience; two, in March 1997, was an Easter Week voyage to the islands of the Southern Caribbean; and three, later in 1997, was a two week, nine island, visit to the islands in the Eastern Caribbean. The Tropicale was the smallest and oldest vessel in Carnival's fleet, at the time, and ended up being sold to the Chinese just like the Love Boat. I preferred sailing on the smaller cruise ships because the better the "passenger to crew ratio", the more personal attention the passengers get. For example, the ratio on the Tropicale was, 1.5:1, that is, for every 1.5 passengers aboard, there was 1 cabin boy, waiter or other member of the crew. Compare this with the situation in 2003, when we were on the maiden voyage of Royal Caribbean's, Mariner of the Seas. The ship had 3000 passengers aboard and was the largest cruise ship afloat at the time. The passenger to crew ratio was almost 3:1 and the lack of individual attention was very apparent. Instead of dressing up and taking their meals in the dining room with their own personal waiter, people began going "topside" in their bathing suits and taking all their meals buffet style. Not my idea of cruising, in style. This is another case where bigger is not always better.

In December, 2000, we sailed the Caribbean on the Costa Victoria, an Italian liner with a completely Italian crew. It was a beautiful ship with wonderful service. It was a Christmas week cruise with hundreds of kids and their parents aboard. I would not recommend doing that to anyone. For the senior citizens aboard, it was much too noisy and clamorous with screaming children running around all over the ship. For the young parents of these children, I would recommend a family style Christmas at home around their own tree, instead of a noisy, public celebration around a huge tree on the main deck of a cruise ship.

While cruising the Caribbean, we visited Saint Maarten twice and found the island a very interesting destination. The island is divided in two, having an unguarded international border separating the Dutch from the French portion.

Cruise ships dock at Phillipsburg, the capital, in the Dutch section. The Dutch part of the island is known for it's festive nightlife, beaches, jewelry, drinks made with native rum-based guava berry liquors and casinos. The Dutch section encompasses the southern 40% of the island and is a constituent of the Kingdom of the Netherlands. The Princess Juliana International Airport, which serves the island is also located in the southern part of the island. The northern 60% of St. Maarten is a French Collectivity, whose capital is Marigot. The French portion of the island is more sedate and is known for it's nude beaches, clothes, shopping and French & Indian Caribbean cuisine. It is also considered a honeymooners paradise. Having enjoyed two visits to this island, we were able to sample most of the features mentioned above.

Another island that we visited twice was, Grenada, the Spice Island in the southern end of the Grenadines. The cruise ship anchored off shore at Saint George's, so we took a launch to the dock. As soon as I stepped foot ashore there, the fresh floral air with a hint of spice energized me. Grenada is famous for its Nutmeg industry. I visited one of the spice plantations there and came home with small bags of nutmeg, allspice, cloves, ginger, cocoa, bay leaves and mace. I went out and purchased a large spice rack, to display them all, when I got home.

Twice, once in the year 2000 and again in 2004, we sailed on a four day cruise from Cape Canaveral, Florida, to Nassau, in the Bahamas on the Sovereign of the Seas. The 2004 voyage was populated by over 100 people from Barefoot Bay to celebrate the 50th Anniversary of priesthood of Father Patrick O'Carroll, who was our pastor at Saint Lukes Catholic Church there. Father "Pat" sailed as the Ship's Chaplain, holding daily Mass, blessing meals etc. These four day, get-a-way sojourns were designed to break up our daily routine. The big attraction there was the Atlantis, a large hotel, casino and entertainment center.

Our stop at Martinique exposed us to the only active volcano in the Caribbean, Mount Pelee located at the northern end of the island. Mount Pelee erupted in 1902, completely destroying the city of Saint Pierre and killing 30,000 people. The city was never re-built and we explored some of the ruins left by that eruption. We examined the bell which had been hanging in the church steeple in the center of town. The heat from the molten lava was so intense, the bell came down from the steeple and melted in a large, distorted mass of metal. Amazing! I saw what once had been a bucket of nails that now looks like a porcupine. Once, on another cruise, when we sailed by the island of Martinique, we saw smoke coming from Mount Pelee.

We made two visits to the Caymen Islands, where the wealthy folks "bury" their money to avoid taxes. We visited the famous turtle farms there.....twice! Sent postcards to our family and friends from

"Hell", a frequently visited village there.....twice! The only thing I did once there, was to rent a Jeep and go sight seeing. On our first visit, with our friends Jack and Eileen Sousa accompanying us, I rented the Jeep and volunteered to drive it. I forgot to mention, in the Cayman Isands, they drive on the right hand side of the road, which is fine until you get to an intersection. Then, you have to remember that left turns are made tight and not wide like in the states. I found myself driving in the wrong lane, against the traffic, at every intersection. Never again!

On the first visit there, I purchased a black coral crucifix with a 14 Karat strip of gold on it, running in each direction, for Georgette. She really loved that cross and often wore it. One day, she noticed that the vertical gold strip was missing. After looking around, we found it in one of the little jewelry boxes in her vanity.. It looked to me as if it had been originally epoxyed in place and the adhesive did not hold up. I attempted to repair it but I was unable to locate a suitable adhesive to do the job. The second time around, we had the presence of mind to take the defective cross with us. The first stop we made after setting foot back in the Cayman Islands, was to go back to Richard's Jewelry store, where the cross was originally purchased. The owner, the one who had sold it to us, acknowledged the problem. He told us that he had a better epoxy, that required a couple of hours to "cure" under ultraviolet light. We left the cross there for repair; returning to pick it up on our way back to the ship for departure. The "fix" is still working.

At each island, Georgette bought a small doll, attired in native costume. She acquired a very nice collection of these and displayed them in a glass-enclosed, etagere in our home at Barefoot Bay. She gave her collection of colorful dolls to our granddaughter, Taylor, when we sold the house.

After visiting all of these islands, I have come to a few conclusions. People say, about the Caribbean Islands, "If you've seen one, you've seen them all." To a certain extent, this is true; almost all of them are lush and green, enjoy tropical weather, numerous beaches and resorts. They all rely heavily on tourism for a stable economy. I have, however, broken them down into two categories: The French Islands; such as, Dominica, Guadeloupe, Jamaica and Martinique, which are occupied predominantly by black people, who are very poor and the slowest to recover from hurricanes and tropical storms because they depend largely on foreign aid that is always slow in coming; and---The British and Dutch islands; such as, Saint Bart's, Antigua, Barbados, Bermuda, Saint Lucia, Grenada, Cayman Islands, Saint Maarten, Aruba and Curacao, which are occupied predominantly by white people, who are not poor and who recover quickly from hurricanes and tropical storms because they do not depend on others to do their job, they repair the damages themselves. The exception to my rule is, Aruba, because it is the only desert island in the Caribbean. All the trees and greenery that are seen on Aruba are imported and transplanted from abroad. Only the aloe grows wild on Aruba.

In our first few years in Florida, we spent a great deal of time enjoying the many attractions around the Orlando area; Disneyland, Universal Studios, Sea World and Splendid China (no longer in business). Orlando is just an hour away by automobile from Barefoot Bay. The Kennedy Space Center, NASA's Operations Center at Cape Canaveral, only a half hour drive, was another of our favorite spots to visit. When our children and grandchildren came to Florida, usually at Christmas time, we would take them to experience these attractions. Because Georgette had become a Florida resident; being senior citizens didn't hurt either, we were able to obtain special rates for ourselves and take advantage of holiday promotions for our guests. It was always my impression that a day at Sea World was the "biggest bang for your buck." If you arrived when the park opened in the morning and planned your itinerary carefully; you were able to visit most venues, have lunch and supper, see the fireworks display and return home shortly after dark. The price, for the day, including parking, was the most reasonable among all the theme parks. These times with our children were both enjoyable and educational for all of us.

Standing in the street, in front of our place in Barefoot Bay, we could see all the space launches from Cape Canaveral. They came into our view just a few feet off the pad and we could watch them lift off and go down range into orbit.

When the shuttles returned, the sonic boom announcing their arrival could be heard, where upon we would go out and watch them come in on the glide path back to the Cape. On January 28, 1986, when the Challenger exploded on take off, killing all seven astronauts aboard, including, Christa McAuliffe, the school teacher from Concord N.H.; we were not yet living in Florida. Georgette saw the explosion of the Challenger, live on TV and called me at work. I had to go home to comfort her because she was so upset. In fact, the explosion was seen in Zephyrhills, on the west coast of Florida, by my wife's sister and her husband. Some one there, with a camera equipped with a telescopic lens, got a shot of the pieces from the explosion flying in the air. In the foreground of that photograph was the American flag waving on a pole in the middle of their trailer park.

I remember a similar occasion, on November 22, 1963, when John F. Kennedy was shot in Dallas, Texas. My first wife, Penny, saw it happen, live on television and she called me at work, as well. I also remember that some of my co-workers at Bell Laboratories actually cheered at the news. I could not believe it! Their president got shot and they cheered. Imagine that! They were over zealous, misguided, conservative Republicans that I was unaware lived and worked among us. I was taught that a person does not have to agree with the politics and decisions of the president, but he must respect the office of the presidency itself. From that moment on, I felt quite differently about those ignorant people who cheered, and I dealt with them differently, as well.

Our bubble burst in 2001, the same year my father died in Jacksonville, FL and the Twin Towers of the World Trade Center came down as a result of a terrorist attack. My wife never got aboard an airplane again. We did take a couple of cruises out of Cape Canaveral, FL, but there was no air travel involved.

Between January 1, 1990 and January 11, 2011, we lived and played in Barefoot Bay, FL enjoying the "Golden Years." After I retired to Florida, I began playing 18 holes of golf 3 days a week: Mondays,

Wednesdays and Fridays. Mondays and Fridays, I was part of foursome which teed off as early as possible; usually between 7:00 and 8:00 A.M. On Wednesdays, it was the Men's League which ran different events each week; such as, Two Man Best Ball, Quota, and Pinehurst.

On Sundays, occasionally I got involved with the Scrambles Event: these were played among teams of 6 or 7 people, men and women. These Scrambles were always very well attended and provided a great deal of golfing fun for a large number of residents and guests. The golf course at Barefoot Bay was a small, 18 hole executive course type layout (Par-60) with 6 Par 4's and 12 Par 3's, but it is very challenging having lots of water hazards and sand traps. I always walked the 18 holes each day up until I was 80 years old, even when the other three guys in the foursome were riding in a golf cart. I do not recommend that as a way to fly, however, because walking behind the other guys in the foursome is very tiresome even when your drives are right down the middle of the fairway.

I should probably mention here that during my early retirement years, I had 2 Holes-in-One! The first was on the 4th of May, 1992 at the Habitat Golf Links in Valkaria, FL at the 3rd Hole (118 yards) using my #7 Iron. The thing I remember most about that hole: from Tee to Green is a swampy, alligator pit from which nobody ever recovered a ball. In the early morning, the golfer is driving directly into the rising sun making it very difficult to see where the ball is going. The second was on the 8th of March, 2004 at the Barefoot Bay Country Club in Barefoot Bay, FL at the 15th Hole (97 yards) using the very same #7 Iron. The thing I remember most about that hole: I was the last driver off the Tee; the other 3 men in the foursome, were already in their golf carts heading for their ball and never saw the shot! Even though I had seen the ball go into the hole, I realized it was going to be very difficult finding a witness to my Hole-in-One. Fortunately, the foursome (4 ladies) preparing to Tee Off on the 11th Tee, which lies adjacent to the 15th Green all saw the ball go into the hole and began yelling and screaming, testifying to the fact that I had, indeed, scored a Hole-in-One.

Another activity with which I became very heavily engaged was slow-pitch softball organized especially for senior citizens. I played every season from the 1989-90 season until the 2010-11 season; that would be between the ages of 59 and 80. The league was originally called the Over 60 Softball League and later became known as the Senior Softball League. Many of these men played well into their eighties and when they were no longer able to run; could receive a "courtesy runner". Each team was allowed 2 non-runners and a list of "designated runners" was generated for each team from which to choose at various situations during a game. I became a designated runner for my team and, of course, I ran for myself for the entire 20 years that I played. We suited 6, and sometimes 7 teams each year with 13 players on a team. In all the years that I played, I was a part of only 2 championship teams. We played 3 seven inning games twice a week, on Tuesdays and Thursdays: rainouts were made up on Saturdays. I also did quite a bit of umpiring as part of a team of three; we took turns behind the plate, at 1st Base and at 3rd Base. Each game day, I would play one game, umpire one game and watch one game. We always played before a large crowd, consisting of wives, friends, families and abutters who sat on aluminum bleachers stationed along the third base line. There were playoffs each year and there were a couple of "All Star" teams that played exhibition games at Dodgertown in Vero Beach, FL prior to the Los Angeles Dodgers spring training games. There was also a "traveling team" which barnstormed all over the state of Florida competing with other teams of seniors from various elderly communities. I played 3rd Base and Left Field for the Barefoot Bay Traveling Team for a while until I was replaced by younger and better ball players.

In 2009, when I was 79 years young, I did something very unusual; I hit an "Inside-the Park" grand slam homerun! The fact that I made the hit was not what was most unusual thing about that event. Where the event took place and the conditions under which it occurred, made it very rare, indeed. It had never been done before and will probably never occur again.

This hit took place in Barefoot Bay, FL during an "Over-Sixty" Softball League game. The ball field there is a small "band-box" sized field with short fields and high fences; all of the home runs sail over the fence into a canal and beyond. It is practically impossible to keep the ball inside the park and still get a home run. Another factor to consider here is that "Over-Sixty softball is played with three short fielders in addition to the usual three outfielders. Let's face it; I could never hit a ball over the fence there. I am a right handed, line drive, pull hitter; who normally pulls the ball to short left field along the foul line. Therefore, the opposition normally overloads the left side of the outfield with fielders. When I began looking for an outside pitch to punch down the right field line, the defense simply stacks people along both foul lines leaving the middle open. It is difficult to go up the middle, however, because the pitcher throws from behind a protective screen about 6 feet high and 4 feet wide; designed to protect him from getting injured from screaming line drives coming off the bat straight back at him. If a batted ball should hit any part of that screen, it is declared a "no-pitch" and becomes a "do-over." On this particular day, I was at the plate with the bases loaded and two were out. I got a good pitch right down the middle which I drove right back to the pitcher, who ducked. The ball just barely cleared the top of the protective screen, bounced just behind second base and skipped all the way out to the center field fence; which isn't really that far, but there is nobody playing center field! By the time anyone was able to retrieve the ball, the bases were clear and I was rounding third and heading home. The throw to the plate was far off the mark and I got the first (and probably the last) inside-the-park home run ever hit at the Barefoot Bay softball field. The fact that it was a grand slam homer was just icing on the cake.

When I first arrived at Barefoot Bay, I played 3rd Base, but I soon became aware that I did not have a good enough arm to throw anyone out. Besides the distance between bases is much shorter on the softball field than it is on a baseball diamond where I was more comfortable. So I found a home in left field, where I was fast enough to go deep for the long ball and come in quickly for the high fly balls over the infield. To compensate for my lousy arm, my shortstop had to come out in left field to serve as cutoff man. There is always somebody at the ball field from approximately 8:30 A.M. until noon, seven days a week having batting practice or a little scrimmage if enough people show up. The Senior Softball League in Barefoot Bay involved a great bunch of guys and their wives/girlfriends and families who were able to recover some of the joys of their youth and to enjoy the comradeship and enthusiasm of other men at the same place in their lives.

In March, 2006, I received an e-mail from my son, Dana, who was working, at the time, for the Tennessee Valley Authority (TVA) at the Sequoia Nuclear Plant in Soddy-Daisy. It read something like this: "Dad, do you know this person—R.P. DePaoli RM3? He was aboard the CV-33 when it transited the Panama Canal and when it was de-commissioned in Bremerton. Washington. I know you were an RM3 (Radioman 3rd Class) and that you were also on the CV-33 on both of those occasions. It seems I've heard this song before." Of course, I knew that guy. He was my shipmate and my best friend for most of my naval career. We went to Boot Camp and Radio School together. We served as radiomen on the USS Kearsarge CV-33 and we did a tour in the Aleutian Islands together. We went on liberty and took our leaves together. We parted company in San Diego during the last few months of our enlistment, when he went aboard the USS Ruddy and I was assigned to the LST-1084. I called Dana back and told him all of the above and asked him where this was all coming from. Turns out, one night at work at the nuke plant, he saw someone on the computer, logged into a site that was displaying pictures and information on WWII aircraft carriers. So he asked if they could enter "CV-33" to see what would come up. Among the stuff that appeared was names of some previous crew members. R.P. Depaoli RM3 was one of those names. That's what triggered his inquiry. Then, I assigned to him the chore of trying to locate him and arrange a meeting. What made the search more difficult and what we didn't realize until much later was that, Bob Depaoli was not the person who made the entry on that site. In fact, he didn't even know that it was there. His son in law, with whom he was living, was the person who had posted his name. I told Dana everything I knew about Bob DePaoli; that he came from Cincinnati, Ohio and his address once was; 2328 Symmes Street. We had to assume that he had married and had children by this time. The trail was very cold for a long time. Finally the scent led us to an address in Lighthouse Point, Florida near Pompano Beach. There was no telephone number listed for that address nor was the name Depaoli associated with it. I assumed that he was living there with a married daughter, who had married a guy with a German name. Dana found an address close by that did have a listed telephone number. He called that number and spoke to a very sympathetic lady who said that although she did not know anyone by that name, she would check on it for him. Dana gave her his cell phone number with instructions to give it to Bob Depaoli if and when she was able to locate him. We figured that was the end of it.

A few weeks later, Georgette and I drove up to Chattanooga for a visit with our kids. As usual, I took us all out to eat at O'Charlie's. We had just finished eating, when Dana's cell phone rang. You guessed it, my old friend, Bob Depaoli was on the other end. It was Saturday, May 6th, Kentucky Derby day and he was at his bookie placing bets on the race The first thing he said to me, "Hey, Baroni, is it really you? What the hell are you working for the FBI or something?" My Italian-American shipmates had nicknamed me, Baroni, years ago to make my name sound more Italian, like theirs. After briefly renewing our friendship, we exchanged addresses and telephone numbers and promised to get together very soon. He was living with his wife, Henrietta; his daughter, Sandy and her husband, Wolfgang in Lighthouse Point; which is a community comprising a network of streets and bridges running by the front of the houses for automobile access to US Route #1 and Interstate 95; and, a network of canals with docks behind the houses for boat access to the Atlantic Ocean. Every house had a swimming pool with a beautifully landscaped patio. The drive between our house in Barefoot Bay and theirs in Lighthouse

Point was about 2 hours right down I95 South. In the next couple of years, we exchanged visits three or four times over lunch and drinks. We were able to re-capture the excitement and thrill of some of our youthful escapades we shared when we were in the navy. Even though we had not seen each other in over 50 years, I am sure we would have known one another had we met in the meantime; we just had not changed that much. During the early days of my retirement, I resumed collecting coins and stamps, specializing mostly, but not limited to, U.S. coins and stamps.

The second Sunday of every month, I attended the Stamp and Coin Show in Melbourne, FL held at the Eau Gallie Civic Center located on Highland Avenue. At one time, I had a very fine collection of U.S. Silver Dollars; including, a very fine collection of all 24 variations of the Peace Silver Dollars, all 32 variations of the Eisenhower Silver Dollars in mint, uncalculated condition, all 12 variations of the Susan B. Anthony Silver Dollars in mint, uncalculated condition, the first 20 years of the Flying Eagle Silver Dollars in mint, uncalculated condition: all mounted in their own special collector's folders. The collection included many Morgan Silver Dollars and a complete collection of Franklin and Kennedy Half Dollars, as well. I sold almost all my coins, stamps and many of my carvings in November 2010, when we were preparing to sell out and leave Florida for good.

One day, while browsing through a crafts store in Cocoa Beach, Florida, I ran across some kits for building doll houses. I had always thought about making one for my daughter or my granddaughter, so I purchased one of the most elaborate kits in the place and spent over two hundred hours building and customizing it. It was a five room layout for which I made most of the furniture myself, including an outdoor patio set with an umbrella. I customized the roof using little, cedar shakes, applying them one at a time. The foundation was a simulated New England style field stone design using plaster-of-paris for the cement holding pretty, tiny pebbles that I picked up at the beach. The completed product was painted two-toned blue and grey and I proudly presented it to, Nicole, my granddaughter, who was about five years old at the time. The doll house was so large, I had to use my Ford pickup truck to transport it from Barefoot Bay to Gardiner, Maine.

Another hobby, which I took up in my retirement is wood carving. I started carving animals, mostly. I never had a lesson; just decided that carving was a good pastime and began doing it. My first carving was a pelican standing on a log. Georgette was into pelicans, having statues of them all over the house in Florida, so I carved one for her collection. I used one of her statues as a model, sketched it on a piece of tissue paper and transferred the sketch to a block of wood. It came out so good that I went out and purchased some books on carving with patterns and instructions. Soon I was making turtles, sea horses, galloping horses, dogs and then Georgette's favorite, an elephant, which I still have in my display case. As I write this story I am still carving. I just finished carving a mermaid which is mounted atop my new walking stick. My next project is a blue heron which I began in Florida some time ago. My second project was a tiger for which I had a pattern that I found in one of the carving books, I just mentioned. I made the stripes on that tiger with a wood burning tool; the first time I ever used a burning tool. A strange thing about that tiger; I never sold it. It is setting on display shelf on my bedroom wall. Every time I attempted to sell my carvings, potential buyers were drawn immediately to that tiger. They would pick it up, admire it; but, it never sold. This has occurred two or three times at yard sales in Florida and again at Hampton Beach and finally, at a couple of craft shows held at Maple Suites in Dover, NH. The tiger is one of my best pieces because it looks so real with whiskers and glass eyes; the first time that I used those two media in my work. The sea horse and the turtle sold the very first time I attempted to sell them to the very first customer who saw each one of them. I never was able to determine which one of my pieces would be the first to sell. I know for sure that the price which I placed upon each piece was never the deciding factor.

During the entire 20 years that I lived in Barefoot Bay, I was a member of Saint Luke's Catholic Church, where I was also an active member of St. Luke's Men's Club. We used to run events; such as, dinner dances in the church hall to raise money for local charities. We ran four or five dances with a catered dinner each year for New Years Eve, Saint Patricks Day, etc. When Joe Valley was our President, we started a new program called Respite. This is a program where volunteers from our men's club would sit for 3 hours each week with "shutin's" to give their care takers a brief rest or respite. Ambrose (Amby) Barry and I used to alternate sitting with a couple of house bound old gentlemen in our community. The care taker would get a chance to go shopping, go to the hair dresser or just go and take a break from their responsibilities. I would sit and talk with the house bound person; watch TV with them, read to them or play cards with them. The Respite Program was well received in Barefoot Bay; we had five or six volunteers relieving a dozen care takers or more. If some one required relief, all they had to do was to go and see Joe Valley or Father Pat.

One day when I was "sitting" with my patient over on South Waterway, I was asked to check the mail. When I went out to their mailbox, I spotted their automobile parked in a driveway about 5 or 6 houses down on the same side of the street. I thought about it for a while, then I understood exactly what was going on. Each time that I came to their house to give his wife some relief, she would go out, get into their car and back it out of the driveway. She would drive off as if she was headed to Roseland or Sebastian, but she only traveled a few houses down the street and pulled her car into the driveway far enough so it could not be seen from their house. She would spend her 3 hours visiting friends and neighbors, playing cards and drinking coffee. Then, when she returned home, she would drive around the circle, entering her driveway in the opposite direction from which she had left. She was fully refreshed and ready for another week of care taking. After a few months of this, I let her know, without actually telling her, that I knew what was going on.

Joe Valley and I are very much alike in many ways. We both lived a "Cursillo," weekend, both served on team and we both gave the "Ideal" talk, which is the most difficult talk for a lay person to give. Joe ran the monthly "Ultreya" meetings at Barefoot Bay and was the President of the St. Luke's Men's Club for many years until he moved up to Daytona Beach for "personal reasons." Ultreya is a monthly reunion for Cursillistas and is held in communities all over the world. The Ultreya format requires that there is a "witness talk" at every meeting; usually given by a former team member or by a Cursillista from another community. I have given the witness talk many times in various locations around the New England area and Florida. I consider it an honor and privilege to be asked to witness and share my religious experiences with others.

Another hobby which I enjoyed over the years was Treasure Hunting with a metal detector; which is an electronic, handheld device that senses the presence of metal, like gold, coins and jewelry. It transmits an audible and visual signal when the search loop detects the presence of metal objects buried in the ground.

I have spent many hours "panning" the beaches of New Hampshire and Florida searching for treasure; coins and jewelry mostly. I still have a metal detector in my closet here at Maple Suites. I built my first metal detector myself along with Sam DiNoto and Pete Tokanel when we working at Bell Labs as technicians. Sam got hold of a schematic of one from a magazine and we designed a package to house it; the most difficult part of that project was "winding" the search coil. It worked pretty well, but it was not nearly as sensitive as we would have liked.

My next detector was a birthday gift from my daughter, Angela and her husband, Dennis. It was a White's; top of the line, in those days. It was very sensitive and it worked well under water. It could locate a penny in the ground over a foot deep! I dropped the control box one day in my shed at Barefoot Bay on the concrete floor and broke it. I managed to get it working, but it never worked well again. One day, my grandson, Jason, and I were treasure hunting at Hampton Beach near my beach house when I received a real strong signal.

I marked the spot in the sand and Jason did the digging with a special galvanized tool which was a scooper and sifter in one unit.

Jason said, "Oh, look Grampy, a quarter!" He cleaned it up and handed it to me; upon examination, I discovered that it was a 1979 Susan B. Anthony silver dollar. The reason why the SBA silver dollar never became very popular was because it was often confused with the quarter; being only slightly larger in size. Another time, Jason and I were "panning" the beach at Jenness State Beach, located a little north of Hampton Beach; when we came upon a "payload" in the sand. The metal detector kept "pinging" and Jason kept digging. Within a couple of square feet, we picked up over two dollars in U.S. coins; pennies, nickels, dimes and quarters and even one half dollar. Some one obviously lost a pocket full of change on the beach while swimming that day. We also found a set of car keys in the sand that day. The lifeguards had gone home for the day, so we turned them in to a policeman on duty near by. In Florida, we lived on the Treasure Coast and treasure hunting was very popular there. People were always finding gold coins and relics from sunken ships from the Spanish Fleet. I used to treasure hunt there along the coast, especially after a hurricane or a tropical storm. Although I did find a lot of things there, I never found any gold coins or valuable relics. One day, after a storm at sea, my granddaughter, Christal and I, had a good day. We found a dollar or two worth of coins and some interesting jewelry in the sand at Wabasso. Another interesting chore for my metal detector, was to help people find items of value that they had managed to lose. In Barefoot Bay, one day at the ball field, Bill Middleton came to ask me if I owned a metal detector. Bill lived right next door to the ball field, along the canal. He had apparently lost his Mason's ring and he wanted me to help him find it. He did not want his wife to know it was missing; she had given it to him as a birthday present long ago. I said that I would help him and went home to get my metal detector. He took me to the exact spot in his back yard beside the canal where he thought he lost it. He told me that he was throwing something into the water when the ring came off his finger and even though he never heard a splash, he thought that it was in the water. I started to search from that spot to the water's edge and within seconds, I got a strong signal: there, in the deep grass, his Mason's ring lay. He was so grateful that I found that ring, we had a little celebration on his lanai over a couple of beers. After that, I was in the business of finding lost metal objects for everyone in the community. On another occasion, at Hampton Beach, Jason and I came upon a young couple having a spat. The young lady had become angry at some point, took off her engagement ring and threw it into the surf. She had a change of heart when we came by and asked us to help them find it. We spent at least an hour searching; never found it. It was at high tide and the surf was churning up the sea pretty badly and must have taken their ring right out to sea. Over the years, I have been asked to help people find all kinds of objects and I was usually successful. I found a metal stake, buried in the ground, which the surveyor's left to mark the boundary of my neighbors property. I have located telephone and cable TV lines, gas and water pipes; until they started using PVC (plastic) tubing. The bottom line is that my Treasure Hunting activities provided me with outdoor exercise, quality time with my grandchildren and the excitement and expectation of finding something of interest or value.

CHAPTER 22

"Autumn Leaves"

During the Summer of 2010, while at Hampton Beach, Georgette came to me and said, "We can't do this any more." I responded, "What is it that we can't do?" She said that we could no longer drive back and forth to Florida each year. I had been waiting for her to make that decision for a long time. Her health had been failing and the trip was becoming more and more difficult for her. I had become her primary care-taker since her Colon Resection operation back in November 2001; then, a Hip Replacement with a metal femur. A Pacemaker installation came next. It was one problem after another until her lungs started to fail and she could breathe no more. The Peripheral Neuropathy had already rendered her practically immobile and she was being treated for Atrial Fibulations (AFIB) and Congestive Obstructive Pulmonary Disease COPD.

I had been doing all of the driving from 1989 to 2010; 21 years. Her incontinence was such that we were unable to pass many rest areas along the way. Since they discovered the Macular Hole in my right eye, I no longer did much driving at night; especially in unfamiliar places. My plan was to locate an Independent Living Community nearby in southeastern New Hampshire; sell the place in Florida, move back to the beach house in New Hampshire and then sell it prior to moving permanently into the new community. Georgette agreed to the plan and I started looking for a suitable location in which to live out the rest of our lives together. I went "on line" and found a site called "A Place for Mom" and called the contact telephone number provided at the site. I spoke, initially, with a lady named, Laura O'Neil, telling her that I was looking for a place for both Mom and Pop. She said that she could definitely help me. I gave her all of our requirements and within the hour; she e-mailed me a list of at least 8 facilities with locations, descriptions, photographs and telephone numbers, for our consideration.

We checked out 3 or 4 of them before contacting Brandy Irish at Maple Suites in Dover, N.H. Brandy came to the beach to learn about us and our needs. Then she invited us to lunch and a tour of the facility. During that tour, I located what I considered to be an ideal apartment for us; one bedroom, first floor, situated close to the Dining Room and Laundry, with two entrances; one to an inside hallway, the other to the outdoor patio and parking lot. After looking around for another month or so, I decided that it was what we wanted. I explained to Brandy that it was still too early for us to make a deposit; we could not afford the expenses associated with living in three places at once. I told her that we were on our way south to Barefoot Bay, where we intended to sell our place there, as soon as possible, returning to the beach house and sell it, as well. Brandy said she would stay in touch and she did.

We returned to Florida in early October, 2010 and I began to play golf and softball, as usual. In early November, Georgette asked me one day, "When are we going to sell this house?" You see, I had forgotten already! I got hold of Pat Webb, a local realtor and put our place up for sale. The very first couple to look at our place, bought it. They did not even attempt to negotiate our "asking price." We sold our home there fully furnished; including curtains, bedding, pots and pans, washer and dryer, dishwasher, everything required to just move in and live. There was even some food left in the freezer! We did not have much time to get rid of a lot of stuff. We took a deposit on November 11, 2010 (Veteran's Day) and closed 60 days later, on January 11, 2011. I ran a constant yard sale from 7:00 A.M. to 7:00 P.M. each day. I placed items for sale in the carport, covering them at night with a tarpaulin. As things were sold and the carport emptied, I just kept filling the emptied space with more things to sell. Some of our neighbors stopped by every day to see what new items I was offering. Some came asking for specific items they did not see but were aware that we owned; which helped us out, as well. We closed in Sebastian on January 11, 2011 at about 11:00 A.M. and headed north with my Buick Park Avenue fully loaded. We traveled one day behind a huge winter blizzard that was churning it's way up the East Coast.

When we arrived at Hampton Beach, the snow was piled higher than I had ever seen it there before. I notified Brandy Irish at Maple Suites that we had successfully sold our house in Florida and that we were back in New Hampshire preparing to sell the beach house in the early Spring. She reported that the apartment we were interested in was still available and that she would keep me posted relative to it's availability. On or about March 1st, I employed our niece, Diane Wasson, who was also a realtor in our area, to sell the beach house for us.

We got a lot of "window shoppers" that Spring and Summer; we got no firm offers or deposits. Each potential buyer had a different issue with our place. It began to look as if we would be unable to sell; even though I dropped the "asking price" to my absolute lowest acceptable price. I was determined not to put Georgette through another Winter at the beach. Between January, when we got back, until March, the winter had already produced mountains of snow, lots of cold and windy weather and very slippery conditions, making it almost impossible for her to get around. She fell a couple of times on the deck trying to get to the car to make a trip to the doctor or to the Laboratory for her INR tests.

One of the Managers at Maple Suites, Harvey Dattoli, was frequently calling me, to inform me that they were showing the unit we were interested in at open houses; that, a great many folks were interested in it and that I should place a deposit on it. I kept thinking; if he was calling ***me***, then no one else wanted that unit anyway. Finally, in late August, he called indicating that he was prepared to offer us some good incentives to buy; to come to Dover and talk it over with him. I answered, "Let's talk on the phone and if we are able to negotiate a deal, then we'll go up to Dover and meet." It was a big job to get Georgette in the car with her Oxygen tank, wheel chair etc. just to meet for a discussion. He began listing some of the incentives he was willing to offer. He said that I would need only a $99.00 deposit instead of a full month's rent and he offered up to $1000.00 toward moving expenses. I said, "OK, go on." Then he offered the first 4 months rent at half price. "Go on," I said; urging him on because I realized that he was determined to sign us up. Finally, he said, "What if I was to offer you a 5 year rent freeze?" My response was, "Write it up, we're on our way!" Georgette and I arrived within the hour to sign the contract. I found out some time later on that there is huge pressure on the managers of these places to obtain full occupancy. Our anniversary date at Maple Suites is August 1, 2011; we didn't actually move in until mid-September. When we moved in, there was a long waiting list for a studio, only a single 1 bedroom unit and 1 two bedroom apartment was available. Maple Suites was 98% occupied; the first and only time ever. This justifies offering potential residents huge incentives to rent.

It works.....They got us for 5 years!

I furnished and decorated the new apartment; had 2 telephone outlets activated and 2 televisions set up with Comcast before we even moved in. I attempted to make the move as seamless as possible. We were in the apartment only 4 days; when I had to pull the Emergency Cord on the wall to initiate a 911 call. The ambulance took Georgette to the Emergency Room (ER) at the Wentworth-Douglas Hospital in Dover where she was admitted. After a brief stay there, she was transferred to Saint Ann's Rehabilitation Center also located in Dover. Then, when her Medicare coverage expired, she was discharged and sent back for home care provided by the Visiting Nurses from Amedysis in Portsmouth, N.H. all covered by Medicare and her AARP Medicare Supplementary Insurance. She was to repeat that cycle every few weeks until she passed away at Saint Ann's on January 23, 2013, only one year and a half later.

In early October, after we were fully integrated into the community, we accepted a deposit on the beach house; and, in

November, we closed on the sale. We were free from all encumbrances of property ownership! My game plan had finally played out!

Soon, I became heavily involved with the residents at Maple Suites. During the first few months, most of my time was spent caring for my wife. I did find time to call Bingo, occasionally and to join the singing group which was called the "Goldentones," at the time. I helped all of the residents who were on Oxygen, like Georgette, to change tanks and to transfer from their Concentrators to Emergency Tanks during power failures. When Georgette was no longer able to take meals in the Dining Room, I carried her food, course by course, from the Dining Room to our apartment, which was located just down the hall.

One evening, I returned to our apartment after supper in the Dining Room at Maple Suites and found Georgette in the bath room struggling to breathe. She said, "Call 911, this is it. I can't do this any more." So I did call 911; the EMT's came in the Dover Fire Department ambulance and took her directly to the Wentworth-Douglas Hospital. When I caught up with her in the Emergency Room (ER), she had this plastic cone over her nose and mouth; one could hear her huffing and puffing all the way down the hall. I had no difficulty finding the Trauma Unit that she was in. She spotted me when I entered the unit and said, "I'm dying, ain't I?" I said that I thought so; I just didn't know what to say. Then she said, "Let me go, just let me go." I did not respond any longer. I was in shock, even though I knew this moment was coming. It took them a long time to stabilize her and to finally admit her to a room located on the 3rd Floor North; The new Garrison Wing had not yet opened for patients. After a week in the hospital, she was transferred by ambulance to Saint Ann's Rehabilitation Center on Dover Point Road. She never came back to Maple Suites again.

Sometime in late November, 2012, Dana and Melissa showed up for a surprise visit from Tennessee. It was a huge surprise because both Mom and I thought we would never see Melissa again. Georgette cried, because she thought that the last time would have been when we drove to Chattanooga from Barefoot Bay for Nicole's wedding. She was still having physical therapy and using her walker to move around the rehab center. Dana noticed that she had slipped back some since the last time he had seen her while visiting her at Maple Suites.

Melissa pampered Mom, painting her nails, styling her hair and dressing her up. The day before they were to return to Tennessee, Christine DeSimone, Jet's Physical Therapist, was going to show her kids how well she was doing. Christine took her down the hall with her walker and Oxygen (O2) level meter with a wheel chair and the rest of us trailing behind. Georgette's O2 level dropped to 78%; she stopped and rested to recover. She did not recover. We had to retreat back to her room with the wheel chair and hook her up to the concentrator. Physical Therapy was suspended; she was never to do any more therapy.

A few days later, when the doctor came to check on her, he ordered her to the Intensive Care Unit (ICU) at Wentworth-Douglas because her lungs were so badly failing. That evening, she called for her husband and a priest. I was nearby, so I came to her side while we waited for a priest. While waiting for the priest, a nurse came in and took me out to answer the telephone. It was someone from Saint Ann's who reminded me that if she made it through the night, there was still a room waiting for my wife there. A new priest from Kenya, Father Patrick, arrived and blessed us both and gave my wife the last rights of the church. Father Patrick was soon to become the Catholic Chaplain for the entire Dover Area. Soon after the priest departed, a lady doctor came into the ICU and said, "She won't make it through the night," and asked permission "to pull the plugs" in accordance with her living will. She was unable to respond, so I gave the "go ahead." What an eerie atmosphere fell over that IC unit! The room became much quieter and much darker; the only sound was her troubled breathing. There was a coned shaped apparatus covering her nose and mouth; which was connected to some kind of respirator on the floor beside the bed. I remained beside her, talking to her all the while, telling her that I loved her; not really knowing whether or not she heard me. Something inside me, said, "She hears you, keep talking; she's listening."

Around midnight, my grandson, Tommy, showed up and took up a post on the opposite side of her bed. Together, we both spoke to her and all the while, Tommy was "texting" to Dana in Tennessee everything that was taking place. She never responded to us, nor did she ever give us a single indication that she was alive. At about 4:00 A.M., a nurse came in to take her off the respirator and hook her up to the O2 supply on the wall through a cannula. Georgette's eyes opened and she said, "Don't take that away, I need it." Then, she looked at me and nodded as if she expected me to be there. She turned to Tommy and said, "Oh, you came! Your father must have called you from Florida and told you to get over here before your Nana dies." That is exactly what had happened!

The next morning at 9:00 A.M., a representative from Dover Hospice, David Vachon, came by to help us exercise our options. Georgette said, "I want to go back home" which meant she wanted to go back to Saint Ann's; her home at the time. An ambulance took her back to her old room, where she was to receive "comfort care" with an extra blanket of coverage from hospice. That meant: no more food or medications, nothing, except 5 Mg of Morphine as required for pain and 2 liters per minute (LPM) of Oxygen (O2) for breathing. The following morning when I arrived at St. Ann's, Melissa Silver, our case worker, offered me a private room at the other end of the hall in which Jet could spend her last days in private. I said, "OK, let's go tell her." As we were going down the hall, I saw her clothes and personal effects already being moved toward the private room. Apparently, Jet had already agreed to the move before I even got there. We got her settled into the new room; she could no longer go to the toilet, so a catheter was attached and a potty chair was set close by. She spent most of the time in the reclining/rocking chair watching the television, at first. She still enjoyed watching her "soaps." Father Don McAllister came every morning with communion; I received as well, when present. Ultimately, he would put a tiny bit of the host on her tongue and I would consume the remainder.

One Sunday afternoon, just about everyone in her family showed up. Her number one son, Billy and his wife, Carla; number two son, George and his wife, Diane; George's son, John; her grandson, William and his wife, CarolAnn; they all appeared without warning. It was as if they were all there for the last time before she died. She knew exactly what was going on; she could have won an Academy Award for her performance that day. She acted like a queen holding court before her subjects. That was the last day she ever sat in that chair. The next day they placed her into the bed; she never got out of bed again. I was spending every day, almost all day in her room with her. Because the hospital "Johnnys" were so uncomfortable, I brought 4 of her pretty nylon nightgowns and cut them up the back so they could easily put them on and remove them. I took the nightgowns home and laundered them myself every other day. Every time, Tracy, the second shift LNA, would change Jet into a clean nightgown, she would transfer her angel pin with a large amethyst on it from one gown to the next. When Georgette passed away, I gave that angel pin to Tracy. Every time I saw Tracy after that, she was wearing Georgette's amethyst angel pin. Georgette spent about 3 weeks in that private room.

On January 22nd 2013, after spending all day at St. Ann's, in that room, I went home to Maple Suites about 9:30 P.M. Shortly before midnight, I got a phone call from Sarah, the 2nd Shift RN at St. Ann's. I knew that something was up because Sarah usually went home at 11:00 P.M. She said, "Skip, you had better get back here. I don't think your wife will get through the night." I told her that I was on my way and hung up. I had to dress up and got back to St. Ann's about 12:10 A.M. Sarah and two 3rd Shift nurses met me and we entered the room where Georgette had spent the last few days. When I reached her side, she was just barely breathing. I spoke to her and told her I was there. I placed my ear right down on her chest to see if I could hear her breathing. I kept talking to her; telling her everything will be all right. I reminded her that she would have no more pain. I got no response from her until shortly before 2:00 A.M. She turned toward me, opened her eyes ever so slightly and said just above a whisper, "I'm afraid."

I told her not to be afraid. Then she said, "You kept your promise." I said, "Yes, of course." She was referring to the promise I made to her forty or more years earlier, when I told her if she stuck with me, I would never leave her, that I would not abandon her, and that I would take care of her and Dana as long as I lived. Then, I said, "If I could, I would go with you." She said, "No, you have to stay and take care of the others the way you took care of me; they need you there." She turned away a little and closed her eyes and never said another word. She just laid there, so still, barely breathing.

At 2:23 A.M., I called for the nurse; she came and I said. "I think she's gone." The nurse left the room; came back with a stethoscope and the other nurse for confirmation. She was gone. I took her wedding rings off her finger and the diamond studs from her ears. It was difficult to do, but the nurses helped me. I took the purple shawl off her; the one our grand-daughter, Taylor, had crocheted for her and folded it up to take home with me. Before I ever completed these tasks, a hospice nurse with whom I was familiar, arrived to prepare the body for cremation. She told me that I had nothing else to do; to go home and they would take care of everything. They did; even notifying Social Security.

Georgette passed away on January 23rd 2013; our son Dana arrived at Maple Suites a couple of days later. George, his wife Diane and I met him at the airport in Manchester, N.H.; we went directly to the funeral parlor in Manchester which was chosen by the National Cremation Society to handle all the funeral arrangements. We became members of that society many years earlier, so everything was prepaid. I was required to sign the necessary documents to permit cremation and to provide the address where the remains were to be sent. I also signed the documents permitting them to remove her Pacemaker and donate it to the Mary Hitchcock Hospital in Hanover, N.H. associated with Dartmouth College.

Then arrangements were made to have a memorial service at Maple Suites on March 8th with Dana presiding. We decided that amount of time would be sufficient to allow everyone to make plans to attend the service no matter where they may have been located on that day. Of course, for some, it still wasn't enough time.

In spite of a snow storm that day, almost everyone got there; even our daughter, Angela, who came all the way from Charlotte, N.C. Dana did a great job with the readings and the homily. The "Goldentones," our Maple Suites singing group, led by Brandy Irish; sang "Be Not Afraid" and "On Eagles Wings." (Georgette had requested these two songs be sung at her funeral.) Stan Jr., one of our Managers, sang "How Great Thou Art" another of her favorites. There was a slideshow which provided many photographs of Georgette's life from about 12 years of age until her death. George and Diane provided five small urns with gold trim into which was placed a small amount of her remains. Her three sons; Billy, George and Dana; her step-daughter, Angela and I, each received one of the urns. A few weeks later, Margie Chamberlain and I deposited Georgette's ashes in the ocean at Hampton Beach near her "rock." Margie recited the prayers while I cast her remains into the surf.

Soon I was calling Bingo 5 days a week, directing the singing group 3 days a week and running a devotional singing session on Sunday mornings. We renamed our singing group, the "Maple Sweets" shortly after Brandy Irish left Holiday Retirement for new employment in Pittsburgh, PA. I also began visiting our residents in hospitals, nursing homes and rehabilitation centers. In a single day, I often visited four different patients located in four separate locations from Portsmouth to Rochester, N.H.

I also became "Mr. Fixit" at Maple Suites and the "Go-To-Guy." I drive people to their doctor, dentist and for laboratory visits. I also drive our residents to wakes and funerals. I fix broken eye glasses, jewelry, watches, television sets, personal computers, printers; anything that can break. I pick up prescriptions at local pharmacies when they are unable to deliver them promptly enough. By the way, there is never a charge for these "services." If anyone slips me cash or leaves it so I will find it later, I put it in my "sunshine fund" envelope. When there are sufficient funds, I go to Dunkin' Donuts early on a Sunday morning and purchase 3 or 4 dozen fresh baked donuts of every shape and flavor and place them on the counter by the coffee urn in the dining room. All the residents get free donuts with their coffee at breakfast and they all get to share the fruits of my labor. When people ask me why I do those things, I tell them that I have been "called" to serve others and that I receive much more than I give.

On January 11, 2015, the Dover newspaper, Fosters Daily Democrat ran a front page story about me; with a color photograph. They called me the "Go-To-Guy" and quoted me as saying, "If it ever worked once, I'll make it work again." Then, on February 22, 2015, I did an interview on the Dover FM Radio Station, WOKQ with Don Briand, who gave me about 25 minutes of "air time" to describe who I am and what I do. Near the end of the interview, he asked me when I was going to stop doing what I do. I told him that I would continue until I am unable, then, I will retire and pray that someone will come along and take over for me. Both of these events were well received by the staff and residents of Maple Suites, as well as, many of the local residents in the Dover area. I get a great deal of satisfaction helping others.

All I need is a hug and a "Thank You" to make my day.

In August 2014, I purchased a brand new 2014 Buick LaCrosse with all the bells and whistles. I said to myself, "This will be the last car I will ever buy."

Then I remembered it was exactly the same thing I said back in 2004 when I bought the brand new Buick Park Avenue. Actually, I owned three new Park Avenues since 1979; paid cash for all three. When GM stopped making the Park Avenue and the Le Sabre, replacing both with the Lucerne, they lost a lot of faithful customers. The Lucerne never did quite cut the mustard. I designed a new vanity license plate for the new car: "&SKIP&" The ampersand represents the musical symbol for a "G Clef." The plate is unique enough to attract the attention of vanity plate buffs who go around taking photos of strange looking license plates and posting them on the internet. I have caught people taking shots of my license plate with their cell phones. I retired my old vanity plate:

"EB+GB"; which no longer seemed appropriate.

In September 2014, I went to my doctor, Dr. Kaminski, in Hampton for a "follow up" examination from my annual physical in March. The news was not good. I stepped on the scale—207 lbs! Whoa, I have never been weighed over 200 lbs in my entire life. Here is the rest of the story: my blood pressure was up, my cholesterol was high; there was no good news. Dr. Kaminski said, "I want to see you in 6 weeks; your weight and other numbers better be down or else." I found my pedometer and began to walk 3 miles a day; 1.5 miles in the morning before breakfast and 1.5 miles after supper. My course consisted of 4 laps around the periphery of the Maple Suites property. My diet was a small bowl of Honey Nut Cheerios with blueberries and a banana, tomato juice and prunes for breakfast. No bread, rolls or deserts and no second helpings for lunch and supper. In 6 weeks, I lost 20 lbs by the doctor's scale and 17 by mine. My blood pressure and cholesterol dropped to acceptable levels. When asked what I was going to do next, I replied to continue to do exactly what I was doing. In 6 months, I leveled off somewhere between 173 and 174 lbs; my initial goal was 175 lbs. I told myself and anyone who would listen, that is my "fighting weight." I have been measuring my weight and my blood pressure on a daily basis since September 16, 2014. I am hovering between 169 and 170 lbs.

Back in the fall, when I began my walking program, I became aware that a resident, Polly, like the parrot, Pelletier and her dog, Sophie, a snow, white Bichon Frise were sitting in a rocking chair on the veranda in front of the building. They were counting my laps and cheering me on. After completing my evening stroll, I would join them and we would sit and chat on the veranda long after the front doors were locked for the night. I knew Polly, and Sophie, for some time as a result of previous encounters and conversations; we were already casual friends. But I did not know that Polly had more than a casual interest in me and she was afraid that I had not yet got over the death of my wife. She was uncertain whether or not I would ever really get over her death because every time I spoke of her, I would fill up and tears would come to my eyes. Shortly after the second anniversary of Georgette's death, Polly and I decided to get together. I was always attracted to her because she is a very fastidious dresser; well color coordinated and she always looks cheerful and carefree. We are well matched because Polly needs someone to look after her and I need someone to care for. I am a talker and she is a good listener. Polly was 79 years old and I was 84 when we decided to hook up. We are both in pretty good health; both of us own a new car and possess a valid drivers license. We are both physically and financially independent. As the saying goes, the rest is history. We have become an item at Maple Suites. The 3 of us can be seen going everywhere together. There have been a few bumps in the road, we are still working things out as we go. Most of our issues deal with the fact that Polly wants 100% of my time and attention. She feels ignored and neglected when I talk for any length of time with anyone else. Being the people person that I am means that just about everyone at Maple Suites gets a piece of me each day. It will take some time for her to adjust to "sharing" me with others.

CHAPTER 23

"Be Not Afraid"

Puzzles

One of my favorite activities is solving puzzles; all kinds of puzzles. I enjoy solving crossword puzzles, cryptos, jumbles, sudoku, rebuses, fill-it-ins, word search etc. I have been solving crossword puzzles since I was about 18 years old. I watched my Mom working crossword puzzles when I was a child. Both of my wives enjoyed working on certain types of puzzles, but I find them all very challenging. When I was traveling all over the country on trouble shooting assignments for Ma Bell, the first thing I would do upon arriving at the airport, was to purchase the morning newspaper and begin working on the puzzles. Some papers carry 3 or 4 different puzzle variations on a daily basis. Most of our local newspapers have the Sudoku, Cryptoquiz and the Jumble, as well as the daily Crossword. I would attempt to solve as many puzzles as I was able before my plane took off. I could usually determine what kind of day it was going to be by the amount of success I enjoyed with solving these puzzles. If I was able to solve all the puzzles posted in the morning paper; that meant I was very sharp and I was in for a very successful and productive day. Of course, if I enjoyed very little success, then I was in for a bad day. Invariably, this became a pretty good "yard stick" for predicting my performance on any given day. I always felt that effort I put into my crossword puzzle solving played a large role with my success at trouble shooting complex problems; both require a great deal of memory and logic. I do possess a better than average memory and I also employ a very logical approach when problem solving. Recently, I have been engaged in group crossword puzzle solving. This is where 6 or 7 people attempt to solve a large puzzle as a team against the clock or against another team solving the same puzzle: the winner having the best time.

My Thoughts on Politics

Politics in my life is an open book. I am and always will be a Democrat. My father and my grandfather were both Democrats. My father was an early union organizer and leader wherever he was employed. When I was a boy, we always bought clothes and goods that were labeled "Union Made"; such as "Fruit of the Loom". I honestly believe that the Democratic Party and organized labor (unions) support the working man; while the Republican Party and "closed union shops" support big business. Big business gives to the working class only what it has to. I also believe that I am my brother's keeper. That is, I should share my good fortune, good health and talents with the less fortunate among us. I do ***not*** believe that everyone on entitlement programs; such as, Social Security, Medicare, Welfare and Veteran's Benefits are "on the take" as most Republicans would have us believe. Nor do I believe that everyone on these programs is sick, lame or lazy. That's what most of my conservative friends, as well as most of my children believe. That is because they never went to bed hungry and cold every night, never had to stand in line for a loaf of "day old" bread or a stick of margarine. I have also learned that these staunch conservatives are first in line to collect these same entitlements when eligible. Think about it, they never voted to support any of these entitlements, but grab them up as soon as they are able. I never heard of any of these hypocrites giving their benefits back either. In conclusion, I am a contributing member, in good standing, of the American Democratic Party and I have been for many years, who believes in putting my money where my mouth is; which is a hell of a lot more than I can say for most Republicans I have ever known. I voted for only one Republican presidential aspirant, Dwight D. Eisenhower (IKE), who actually won as we all know. In local elections, I do not vote the straight party ticket. I will always consider voting for the best candidate when the choice becomes critical. The greatest presidents in my lifetime have been Franklin Delano Roosevelt

(FDR) and John Fitzgerald Kennedy (JFK). Finally, I believe we must put down all the greed in the world and learn the art of being good to one another. People who say, "I've got mine, to Hell with everyone else," have got to go!

Family Discipline

There is a tradition in my family which pertains to discipline. The tradition revolves around a person or thing known as, "Dr. Bokackiac," pronounced just the way it looks, which hangs on a hook in a prominent place in our home, normally in the kitchen. Actually, Dr. Bokackiac is nothing more than an old, man's belt with the buckle removed. Whenever a child misbehaves, he or she may be "introduced to the doctor." Just the mention of his name or a threat of being introduced is all that is required. Dr. Bokackiac has been in my family for at least 3 or 4 generations. I have seen or felt it being applied twice in my life. The "introduction" is usually two or three brisk strokes on the bare behind accompanied by a lengthy lecture explaining exactly why this has been necessary. This may seem like cruel and abusive treatment, but I will testify to it's effectiveness. Just the presence and the threat of being used is 99.9% effective. I have never heard anyone else in my entire life ever even mention the name, Dr. Bokackiac.

My Thoughts on Religion

Religion in my life has always been an "on again", "off again" thing. Whenever I get off track; somebody or something appears to take me back "home". I was baptized in the Catholic Church at birth, which was a rather typical start. The only odd thing about that was, at the time, my father was a non-practicing Catholic and my Mom was a Protestant. No way, you say: never heard of an Italian girl who was not Catholic. Turns out that some of my Mom's siblings were Catholic and some, evidently, were not. Apparently, religion was not a huge factor in their family. My Mom converted to Catholicism when she married my father. That explains why I did not make my First Holy Communion until I was 11 or 12 years old. My 4th grade public school teacher came forward and saw to it. I was not confirmed in the Catholic Church until September, 1954 at Saint Joseph's Church in Salem, NH, two months after I was married there. I had to promise to be confirmed with the children, because, according to Father Dolan, pastor at the time, "No one gets married on the altar in my church if they have not been confirmed." All of the parishioners at St. Joe's thought that I was "something else" that day. Needless to say, there were a great many "on again" and "off again" times between my First Holy Communion in 1940 and Confirmation in 1954. Probably, the first "turn off" occurred when I was about 15 years old. I was in high school and attending Saint Rita's Church in Haverhill, MA and playing basketball for St. Rita's; we had a team competing in the City Church League and the Catholic Youth Organization (CYO) League that year. In order to play for St. Rita's, I was required to be a member of the church, of course, and also to attend all the religious training classes; such as, bible study and Confirmation preparation classes. One Saturday, in the confessional, Father Piscatelli told me (who said the priest doesn't know who you are in the confessional), that he would not grant me absolution nor would he allow me to play basketball for St. Rita's unless I began attending bible history and Confirmation classes immediately.

I left the confessional that day and did not return for many years. I did, however, begin attending bible history classes and continued until the basketball season was over; at which time, I stopped going to church period. We won the CYO League title that year as well as the City League title. I never played basketball again or even went to church until I was in the U.S. Navy in 1949.

When I arrived in Boot Camp at Great Lakes, IL; while stamping out my "dog tags", a "C" was stamped in the appropriate location to identify me a Catholic. That event automatically provided me with an interview with the base chaplain.

Upon learning that I had not yet been confirmed, the priest said, "You will be confirmed here at Great Lakes while going through your boot training."

My response, "Wanna bet!" It did not happen!

A few months later, when I was attending U.S. Navy Radio School in Norfolk, VA, two of my best buddies from boot camp who were also going to radio school with me, Bob DePaoli from Cincinnati, OH and Bill Spurge from Brooklyn, NY, got on my case. No matter what occurred on Saturday night, these two guys would get me out of the rack every Sunday morning and drag me off to Mass at the base chapel. You guessed it….I was on again! After Radio School, I was to serve on various ships and stations, and again, stopped going to church for whatever reason. Fast forward to 1951 or 1952, I was stationed on Attu in the Aleutian Islands: the only Radioman in hundreds of miles; also serving as the Mailman, Tide Gauge Operator, Control Tower Operator and Harbor Master. A military aircraft flying between Japan and the United States on the great circle route, called asking permission to land on Attu. Apparently, the plane was scheduled to set down at Shemya AFB; but Shemya was socked in with bad weather. This was a normal situation; when the field at Shemya was socked in, Attu became clear for landing and vice versa. So I talked the plane down on Attu using Visual Flight Rules (VFR). The plane taxied up and after the pilot complimented me on providing good landing instructions, a full bird Colonel in the US Air Force disembarked, who just happened to be a Catholic priest. He was the same priest who used to run the "Catholic Hour" on radio station WCKY from Cincinnati OH when I was in grammar school. This guy asked me if I was Catholic, handed me a small satchel which contained his holy wine, chalice and materials for conducting Mass and told me to round up all the Catholics on the island and to get prepared to hold Mass in the library ASAP. He said, the Mass would be preceded by confessions. There were about 60 men on the island at the time; maybe 27 of whom were Catholics. None of us had seen a priest in 2 years or more. We all went to confession sitting in a corner of the library on a chair, facing the priest while he held both of our hands in his own. This was the most complete and exhilarating contact with God I had experienced up to that point in my life. You have to know that I was "on again."

I left the Aleutian Islands, served out the rest of my enlistment on the USS Bellatrix AKA3 and the USS Polk County LST1084 before I was honorably discharged. I stopped going to church again, except on special occasions; such as, Easter and Christmas.

I was "off again" until 1954 when I got married to my first wife in St. Joseph's Church in Salem, NH. In 1975, my 2nd wife, Georgette and I were regularly attending Mass at Mary, Queen of Peace Church also in Salem, NH and our son, Dana, was preparing for his Confirmation. We got heavily involved with the "Renew Program" there. The first year, Georgette and I attended the sessions, one night per week for 12 weeks at the home of Joan and Dick Palmer. The second year, we met at our home on Glen Denin Drive. I was the facilitator and my wife, Georgette was the hostess. Usually, we sang hymns, read scripture, had intense discussions and ended the evening with a coffee and cake social. We had seven married couples and one nun who came quite regularly. This activity provided everyone with many benefits. Georgette got over her shyness and difficulty dealing with new people. That group of people became very dear friends and the ones who are still alive, have remained in touch with each other over the years. From this group of people, we were introduced to the "Cursillo Program"; which was kind of weekend retreat being held at the time at St. Basil's in Methuen, MA. Since living the Cursillo, I have been "on again" for good! I witnessed miracles and healings and watched alcoholics become sober.

In fact, Georgette got healed on her weekend at Saint Basil's.

A "Cursillo" is actually similar to a "Retreat", but more so. You are sequestered over a weekend: from Thursday evening until Sunday evening, without benefit of television, radio, telephone, clocks, watches or a calendar; complete isolation from the outside world. During the entire weekend, you are being supported and all your needs are supplied by a team of your peers. I "lived" my "Cursillo" weekend in December, 1980 and Georgette "lived" hers in January, 1981. I have also served on a team, where I delivered the "Ideal" talk, which is one of the most difficult talks given by a lay person over the weekend. Men and women live the weekend separately; the men go one month and usually, the women go the following month. This sequence occurs about five times per year. In Spanish, the word "cursillo" means a short course in Christianity; according to my old friend, Father Joe Dagher. Father Joe was one of the best priests and one of the greatest guys I have ever known. Those who have lived the weekend are called "Cursillistas" and the greeting which is employed when one "Cursillista" meets another is: "Des Colores". Perhaps you have seen that expression on a vanity license plate or on a decal somewhere. I learned a great deal from Father Joe and he was a huge influence in my religious life. People would come to him and say, "Why is God punishing me?" Father Joe would respond, "God does not punish us, we punish ourselves!" Think about that for a moment. He was not a big fan of the "fire and brimstone" preachers who are always harping on the the "letter of the law." He would frequently announce, "The letter of the law…… kills. The spirit of the law…..lives."

One day, I had stopped at Golick's Ice Cream Stand on Dover Point Road in Dover, to buy an ice cream cone; when I met a young boy about 10 years of age who was sharing the picnic table with me along with a few other children. While I was conversing with the children, this young man asked me, "Do you think that God is a woman?" While I was pondering for a response, I was wondering what had provoked such a question. I started first with the Trinity and the explanation of the concept of three persons in the one God; the ***Father***, the Son and the Holy Spirit. Not the Mother, but the Father, being a man, and therefore of the male gender. I went on to explain that in most modern day religions, God is thought to be a man, and that the only woman frequently admired and worshipped, is Mary, the Mother of God. I went further to explain that, since God is considered by most to be omnipotent, there is no reason why God should be confined to any specific gender. I am not sure whether or not the boy bought my explanation, but he seemed satisfied. I am often upset by Christians, mostly, who pick and choose what they want to believe about God. The virgin birth, for example, is not accepted by all believers. I say to them; If you can believe, without any reservation, that God created the entire universe and all that is in it in 6 days; what is your problem? The virgin birth is a piece a cake for God; remember, all things are possible with God, including perhaps, something like creating the big bang theory?

This part of my life story would not be complete without sharing my thoughts on Heaven and Hell; what happens to our body and soul when we die. First of all, I do not believe Heaven is a "place" way up in the sky somewhere; a paradise where, your soul floats around for an eternity. Rather, I think of Heaven as a state of mind, or of the soul; where our soul finds eternal rest and peace. As for Purgatory; defined as, a place or state of the soul where sinners go to expiate their sins before going to Heaven; a kind of "half-way house." I don't think so! Same goes for Limbo; defined as, an abode of the souls of unbaptized infants and pagans, a kind of "no-where land." Again, I don't think so!

The God I know, did not make achieving Heaven so complicated.

I firmly believe ***all*** souls either go to Heaven or they don't, whether or not they are "born again.!" Where do they go when they don't go to Heaven?

I definitely don't believe that Dante Alighieri's Inferno (Italian word for Hell"), the first part of his epic poem Divine Comedy; accurately describes where and what Hell really is.

My Mom used to say, "Hell, is right here on earth." She certainly experienced enough suffering and pain in her lifetime to justify that statement. I know for certain, if indeed, there is a Heaven; her soul is resting very peacefully there. What about the body? What happens to it? The expression "ashes to ashes and dust to dust" is frequently used at many funerals.

Don't look for that phrase in the Bible because it just isn't there! The closest thing to it can be found in Ecclesiastes 3:20 or Genesis 3:19; "By the sweat of your face you shall eat bread, till you return to the ground, for out of it you were taken; for you are dust, and to dust you shall return." I believe that the spirit or soul of man will live beyond the grave, but not so with the body, it will turn to dust.

The most profound poem I have ever heard, "The Touch of the Master's Hand" by Myra Brooks Welch, terminates my section on Religion. My brother, Buddy, introduced me to it back in 1976 at my daughter, Angela's wedding.

A "mess of pottage", a glass of wine;
A game—and He travels on.
He's "going" once, and "going" twice,
He's "going" and "almost gone",
But the Master comes, and the foolish crowd
Never can quite understand
The worth of a soul, and the change that's wrought
By the touch of the Master's hand.

My Medical Issues

Early in my career at Western Electric, the company used to provide a very extensive annual Physical Examination. At first, this was done off campus by a local physician chosen and paid for by the company. Later, it was done, in our own in house laboratory, because we had obtained a full time company doctor, a team of nurses and a well equipped hospital. Because we were self-insured, all these facilities made good sense. During one of these examinations, an extensive blood panel was done which included Hemoglobin and Hemochromatosis genetic tests. These tests revealed a condition known as, Thalasemia; which is a genetic disease that results in the production of an abnormal ratio and size of hemoglobin sub-units. The test was done a few times since the first revelation, but the numbers, expressed in parts per million, did not change over time and no action was ever taken. I later learned that my daughter, Angela, also had Thalasemia, as well as some kind of anemia dealing with iron deficiency It was revealed to her during her first pregnancy, Jason; while performing pre-natal blood testing. Since this condition is genetic, my Angela obviously got it from me. Further research revealed that Thalasemia is most prevalent among people coming from the Mediterranean Region of Europe. Since my grand-parents came from Italy, I must have inherited it from my mother. There is no cure for this condition and it is not fatal. I have another unusual condition which was discovered in 2003 by Dr. Harish Sadwani in Sebastian, FL, during an annual physical examination. Georgette was going to his wife after her Colon Resection operation and I was going to the husband. They were both practicing out of the same office. After receiving what I thought to be a very unusual type of EKG Test in his office; I was lying there for a long period of time waiting for the results. The doctor finally came in and asked me if I had ever been told that I had a Right Branch Bundle Block. Of course, I said, "No." He described the condition as being more of a concern with the "electrical" system rather than the "plumbing" system of the heart. In other words, the blockage was not dealing with blood clots in the arteries. The doctor scheduled an extensive stress test performed on a treadmill; while some comprehensive monitoring was done. I was told the condition was not fatal; I guess the Left Branch knew what to do when the Right Branch was blocked. I never heard anything about bundle blocks until a few years later; a fellow named, Joe Cummerford, who played softball and basketball with me when we were both working for Western Electric/AT&T, passed away from a Right Branch Bundle Block. He died very shortly after we had accepted an early retirement package and his death was a huge surprise because he was much younger than I.

In the summer of 2008 or 2009, my wife Georgette forced me to go to the Emergency Room (ER) at the Exeter Hospital because I was experiencing some kind of heart palpitations. These erratic heart beats were so loud, they could be heard by people standing by. After a number of heart tests, it was determined that I have a condition called, Arrhythmia, described as an irregular heartbeat. The condition is considered non-fatal and I was treated with medication, Verapermil 240 Mg, which I still take daily.

EPILOGUE

I am probably one of the richest people on earth. I have my family, my health, my friends and I am still living a productive, meaningful life. All the things that money cannot buy. As long as I am still alive, of course, my story is not over. I will not apologize to anyone for anything that I have said here because it is both truthful and accurate as seen through my own eyes. My story proves Dr. Massey's theory: "You are what you are because of what you were when." Another thing I learned: as Tony Bennett says in his book; Life is a Gift: "You cannot plan your life; your life plans you." As I reflect back over my life, I am reminded of Frank Sinatra singing the song, My Way: "To think I did all that; and may I say, not in a shy way, I did it my way!"

Always remember: The more you go back, the more you move ahead!

ACKNOWLEDGEMENTS

I would like to thank Marjorie Chamberlain for her unwavering support and faith along with her expert assistance editing and proofreading this book. I wish to acknowledge Monique Foote, my personal friend and "manager" for her encouragement and support which motivated me to finish writing my story. Finally, I must recognize Polly Pelletier (and Sophie) for their patience and understanding throughout the entire process.

Mom & Skippy 1935
Lake Attitash, Merrimac, Ma.

Skippy with "Robin" 1937

My Father w/ "Flash" 1937
Grampy Biron with "Tarzan"

My Dad at 90 October,1998
Jacksonville, Florida

Skip's 1st Car *1946 Mercury Conv.*

Haverhill High School 1948
EJB Year Book Picture

Skip 1954

Skip Biron Rm3 1951

Skip Biron Engineering Associate 1972

Can you identify the top photo? Write your guess and any comments on a post card and mail to Thanks for the Memories, Haverhill Gazette, Post Office Box 991, Haverhill MA 01831. Last week's photo was of the Capovilla AC basketball team, as shown on the jerseys. The challenge was in the date and names. This was taken in 1947, when the Capovillas won the YMCA Community League title.

Front, from left: Jim Scorsoni, Skip Biron, Donald Shaw, Bob Conte, Assistant Coach Charles Pento Sr. Back, from left: Coach Ed "Diddy" Biron, Pat Cagnetta, Charles Kimball, Joe Bolter, Wayne Grazio. The photo was submitted by Wayne Grazio, who said the games were played in the old YMCA gym on Main Street, next to the present City Hall, which was formerly Haverhill High.

The only correct answer to arrive before press time was from Bob Conte, who was in the front row of the picture. He had the date and all the names. If you have any photos you think might be of interest, please send them to Barney Gallagher at the above address.

Coach "Diddy" Biron, Jim Scorsoni, Dick O'Neil, Nick Abate, Bob Carozza
Wayne Grazio, Don Amaro, Skip Biron, Bob Conte, Pat Cagnetta

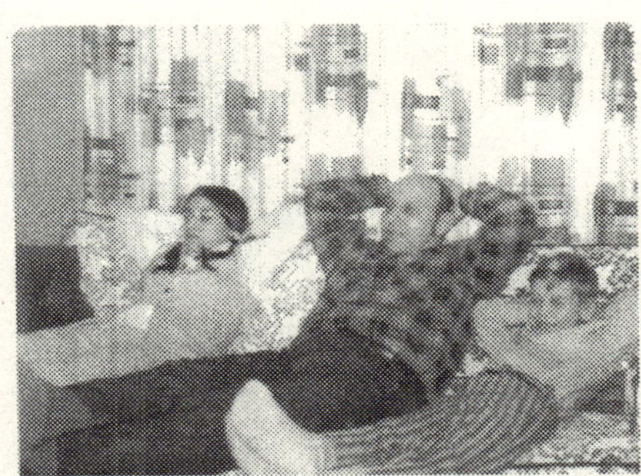

Angela (12), Skip (38) & Dana (4) 1968
Georgette's Living Room Methuen, Ma.

Buddy, Daddy & Skip 1969
VFW Methuen-Memiere's Funeral

Kerry, Terry, Barry, Lisa, Laurie
Skip Norma
All Birons at Daddy's Funeral April 2001

M y Sister, Norma-1959
17 Years Old

NOB ATTU, Alaska 1951

Jap Field Piece ATTU 1951

Navy PBY on Runway-ATTU

Bob DePaoli

ADAK, Alaska 1951

Skip Biron

Scenic ATTU in 1951

USS Bagaduce ATA-194 (Took us fm Attu to Shemya- Bob Hope Show-1951

USS Namakagon AOG-53 (Took me from Adak to San Pedro, Ca.-1952

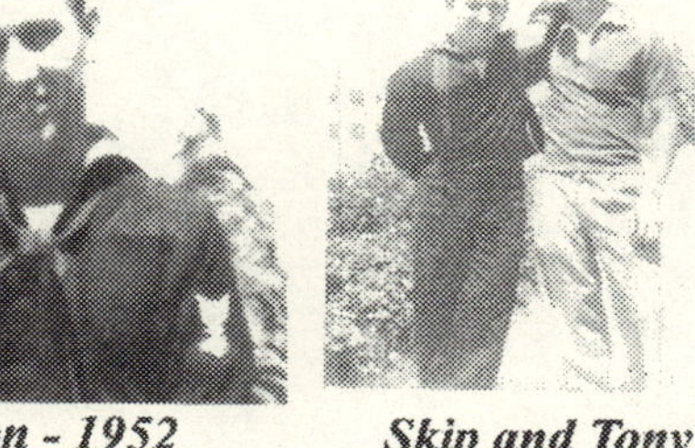

Skip Biron - 1952 ***Skip and Tony*** ***Skip Biron 1952***

Taken in Long Beach, Calif., When stationed aboard USS Bellatrix

Skip in Civies
1952

Skip in Uniform
1952

USS Kearsarge CV-33 in Port-au Prince, Haiti - May 1949

USS Belatrix AKA-3 in San Pedro, Ca. - March 1952

USS LST-1084 in San Diego, Ca - August 1953

EE Award Nite Andover CC

Georgette and Skip 1972

Engineering Excellence Citation

Ed Biron with Mr. Hilder 1972

MERRIMACK VALLEY WORKS ENGINEERING EXCELLENCE PROGRAM

CITATION

Without a doubt, an award winner must have technical ability, [illegible], experience and leadership.

All of these should be coupled to good attitude and willingness to devote long hours to bring every project to a successful end.

That is what has been said and written many, many times about this award winner.

Our man, not only proves his ability and leadership when summoned to the field, by "gently" but firmly guiding everyone connected with a trouble system, but also at the Merrimack Valley Works he shines for his accomplishments. A few examples will suffice to clearly indicate the impact he has fostered upon the MV Works.

His numerous publications include an article for the "Western Electric Engineer" - concerning his Time Domain - Reflectometry Technique. And to show his versatility, he designed the front cover for that issue.

His publications and technical literature have been designed to acquaint, describe, instruct. These have been of great help to those who have to work with the projects assigned to him.

He received a SILVER MEDAL award for co-authoring an outstanding paper at the 11th TEST ENGINEERING CONFERENCE.

He has earned reputation for solving the diversified problems affecting our equipment when interfaced, here and in the field, with other manufacturer's equipment.

Keeping alert for innovation, he is the joint owner of the US Patent titled: SYSTEM FOR [illegible] A SIGNAL.

This self-made man is never satisfied with mediocre performance. He is never hampered by the thought of "it can't be done" or "it can't be fixed". He is [illegible] a very determined man for a job well done. Perhaps a more meaningful tribute can be summed up by a poem written by a [illegible] Engineer - pertaining to a system which for some reason could not be made to work. The last four lines simply state:

> HOURS BECAME DAYS AND DAYS BECAME WEEKS AT [illegible]
> SOMEONE SUGGESTED: LET'S PLACE A CALL TO MERRIMACK VALLEY
> THE CALL WAS MADE, NOT UNDER DURESS
> AN ASSOCIATE CAME AND CLEANED UP THE MESS

Mr. Hilder - that Engineering Associate is our award winner - ED BIRON.

MR/MRS ED BIRON ANDOVER CC 1972

JANUARY 1972

Western Electric

The ENGINEER

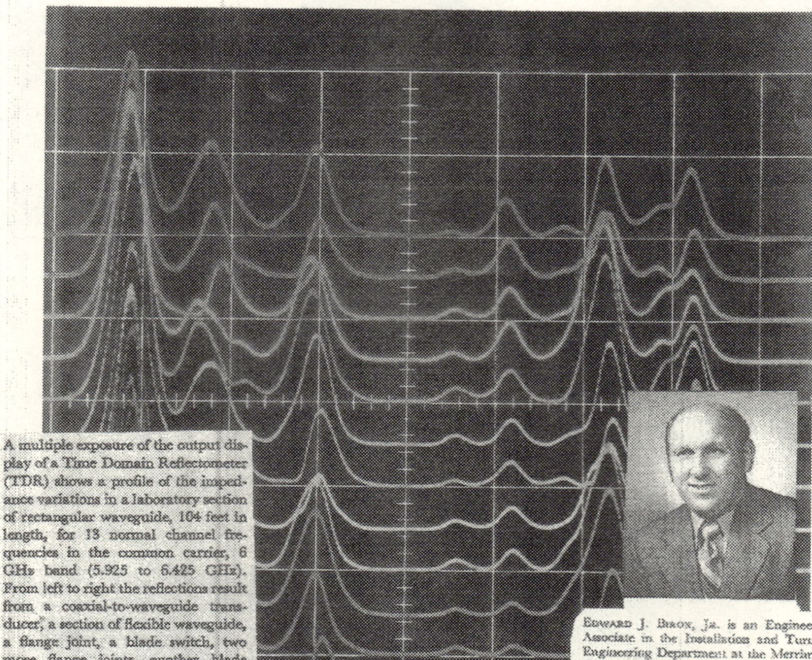

A multiple exposure of the output display of a Time Domain Reflectometer (TDR) shows a profile of the impedance variations in a laboratory section of rectangular waveguide, 104 feet in length, for 13 normal channel frequencies in the common carrier, 6 GHz band (5.925 to 6.425 GHz). From left to right the reflections result from a coaxial-to-waveguide transducer, a section of flexible waveguide, a flange joint, a blade switch, two more flange joints, another blade switch and finally the end termination or load. The trace colors were added in processing and were chosen to represent the relative frequencies in the 6 GHz band used for this test. With TDR techniques the magnitude and location of each reflection can be directly determined. Cover photograph was made by Charles Lewis.

EDWARD J. BIRON, JR. is an Engineering Associate in the Installation and Turnkey Engineering Department at the Merrimack Valley Works. He joined Western Electric in 1953 after serving 5 years in the U. S. Navy as a radioman. After working in carrier and filter testing and test set maintenance, Mr. Biron spent 10 years on loan to the Bell Telephone Laboratories as a test set technician. In 1966 he assumed his present assignment which involves testing, analysis and alignment of multi-hop microwave communications systems. Mr. Biron also holds a patent on the method of pulse modulating a signal described in this article.

The BOYS of WINTER

Top Row-Rene Segoin, Ben Becker, Jim Gangone, Bill Shields, Mike Mekanko, Lou Smith, Cliff Gallant Bottom Row-Leo Oulette, Tony DiFazio, Amby Barry, Skip Biron, Charlie Simpson and Phil Miller

Abbott Homes was the team to beat in the Over 60 Softball League this season, but no one did, and they went on to become league champions, in addition, Abbot Manager, Mike Mekanko, was named the league Manager of the Year and Billy Shields the Most Valuable Player. Congratulations to Abbot Homes on their fine performance. See you all next year! (From the Barefoot Tattler May 1997)

Skip Biron-1997

Skip Biron- 2001

First Union - Barefoot Bay Over 60 Softball League Champs 2001-2002

Skip Biron- 2000

Skip Biron- 2003

5 Room Doll House /w Patio Built for my Granddaughter, Nicole -1993

Skip's First Carvings--Made in Barefoot Bay, Florida--1996-2008

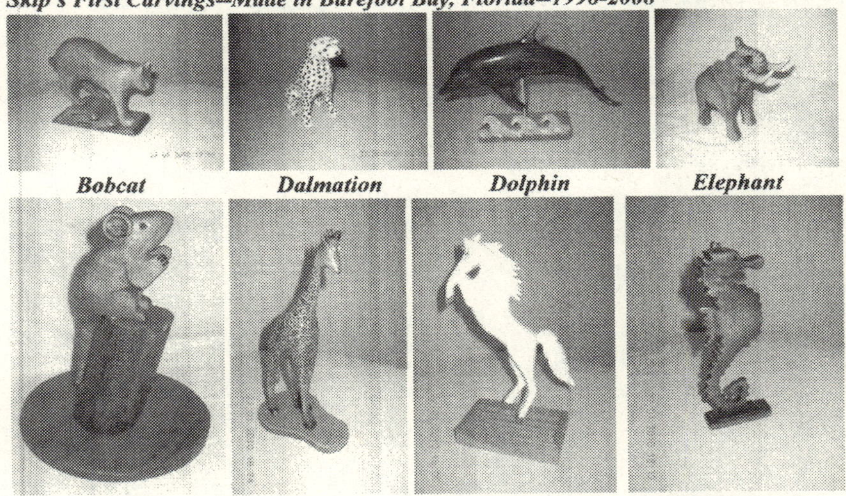

Pelican A ***Quarter Horse*** ***Turtle***

Shark ***Tiger*** ***Pelican B***

Golden Retriever ***Great Dane*** ***Ceramic Chess Set Special Board/Table***

Ceramic Xmas Tree (Gift from Jeanette) ***Lighted Christmas Village by Skip 1998***

Fosters Daily Democrat-Jan 11, 2015-Front page picture of Skip Biron and story, "Senior & Wired"

Dover, NH FM WOKQ Feb. 22, 2015 Skip Biron Interview /w Don Briand

Skip's Walking Stick
He carved the mermaid handle at Maple Suites in early 2015.

Printed in the United States
By Bookmasters